Misunderstood

Misunderstood

by

Nicole K. MacIntyre

ISBN 978-1-257-88600-5

To my brother and parents for standing by my side and helping me through.

Table of Contents

Trapped

Judgment

"It's their fault they're anorexic. It was their choice."
"Anorexics don't eat at all."
"Anorexics just can't find a better way to lose weight."
"They only care about looking good and being skinny."

These are some of the stereotypes that are often spoken about anorexia. These are the same stereotypes that I once believed not so long ago. Like many of you, I would read about the newest anorexic Hollywood star and be disgusted. *How could she do that to herself?* I asked, *Why would she ever be that desperate to get skinny?* But fast-forward a year and it's no longer the anorexics who disgust me; it's the people who stereotype them who I find myself scowling at.

We all hear cliché phrases such as "Don't judge a book by its cover" and "Try walking a mile in their shoes," but until recently, I didn't realize how true those phrases truly are. I had to go through the pain, the struggle, the agony, and the battle. It's a beast that has sent my life spiraling out of control. Anorexia is a deep, emotion-packed disease; stereotypes that anorexia is fueled by vanity could not be further from the truth.

The most exasperating statement I hear on a daily basis is that this was my fault. I can assure you that this year—this journey—has been the hardest struggle anyone in my family has ever faced. Never did I think things would get this bad. Never did I realize what was happening to me until it was too late. I can honestly tell you that I believed myself to be normal. That's what many people don't understand: The actions anorexics take and the statements they say clearly lead to one simple answer. How can they not realize they are anorexic? Again, it's the lies of the disease. Every piece of food I don't eat and every pound I lose only makes me feel stronger. And when others around me desperately attempt to shake me out of it, all I can think is that they are the crazy ones, not me. In my mind, I'm just losing some harmless weight and what I'm eating isn't much less than before. In my mind, my parents are overreacting and my friends are just jealous. In my mind, the doctors just want me to be fat so there's no need to listen to their petty advice.

When first sucked into an eating disorder, what the eating disorder tells you is law above everything else. I became trapped. There were no other options. I was caught, and listening to my eating disorder seemed to be the only way. But if I could've fast-forwarded in time, if I could've seen where it was heading, what I would encounter, then maybe I could've stopped myself. I could've seen the truth and avoided the pain.

Truthfully, I didn't even want to lose weight. Well, maybe just a couple pounds but nothing drastic. No, weight loss was not my motivation. What I yearned for was control. Control over an unruly matter. Control over food and weight and how I looked. Control would mean I had power. Control would mean I was strong. And that was all I wanted. I was sick of getting through every day feeling as though I wasn't good enough. There was nothing special about me, nothing to set me apart.

There were three of us at the time. It was me and my two best friends. Susan was the skinny one, the pretty one, the smart one. Everywhere I went I heard people talking about how nice she was or how they wish they had her body. Boys liked her. Girls loved her. And I was just the best friend. It wasn't much better with Claire. She was the funny one, the outgoing one, the one who always managed to find a boyfriend. She was hardly ever single and she was always meeting new boys. And I was just the best friend. Even worse, I saw myself as the ugly one, the worthless one, the annoying one.

My self-esteem was about as low as it gets. Although I acted happy and plastered smiles on my face everywhere I went, there was nothing but depression and helplessness lying underneath. Restricting foods made me feel proud of myself. I never felt proud. I was never strong. I was never in control. Once I found a way to achieve the desired feelings, I couldn't stop. Every time I was put down or made a mistake, the restricting only got worse. It quickly became an addiction. It seemed every little thing that went wrong had a simple solution: eat less or exercise more.

Lent

We are a Christian family. Protestant, not Catholic. Not once in my life do I remember our family participating in Lent. In fact, up until about seventh grade, I didn't even know what Lent was for. Even by eighth grade I hadn't fully grasped the concept.

But that March, I spent my weeks listening to friends discussing the start of Lent and what they were going to give up. For some it was chocolate. For some it was any and every sweet. For some it was soda or sugary juices. No matter who was talking, the items they chose to ban until Easter all had one obvious similarity: they were all giving up some sort of junk food. All trying to be that much healthier and signaling their devotion to God by choosing not to give in to temptation. An idea came to me. Recently, I too had been resisting food temptations. But having no reason for doing so, I found myself still munching on sweets every now and then. This would be my chance. This was my opportunity to prove how strong-willed and in control I could be. This would be the way to prove to myself that I could live without sugar. This was a test. A test to see how determined I really was. If I failed to keep my commitment then I deserved the insults I gave myself. But if I somehow managed to make it through then, perhaps, I was a better than I thought.

Telling my mom of my decision to cut out chocolate and not drink soda was a success. At first, she seemed a bit surprised. In response, I told her I had a need to worship God and live a more healthy life. She said she was proud of me, and went on to say it'd be great if I could give up sodas for good.

Yeah, I thought, maybe I will. Maybe this is the beginning of a stronger, smarter Nicole.

Carrying this thought, I floated off to bed with a smile plastered to my face. As the weeks went by I found myself amazed at how easy the restricting turned out to be. Saying no to sweets wasn't hard and it definitely didn't make me feel upset. In fact, it was just the opposite. Each time I resisted my urge for chocolate or my desire for soda, a wave of power flushed through me. It made me overflow with happiness as I received praise from those around me and best of all, praise from myself.

I had never praised myself. And by never I don't mean occasionally or not that often. I mean never, as in, every day, every minute, I had nothing but criticism. And let me tell you, praise felt good. It felt like I was finally the puppet master instead of the puppet. No more being controlled by food. No more making unhealthy choices. I was in charge and I loved it.

Unfortunately, as time went on, I strived for more and more control. I rejected more and more foods, and when Lent finally ended, I didn't stop. I did return to drinking soda but with one exception. Diet was the only kind I could have. No sugar, no calories, perfect choice. And not only did I stick to my "no chocolate" rule, but I added to it as well. The list of rules quickly piled up. There was no ice cream, no pizza, no french fries, and no bagels. It didn't stop there. Rules consisted of more exercise, less sitting around, and the need to weigh myself at least once a day.

As the rulebook grew and my weight began to drop, I felt as though I was more in charge of my life then I ever had been before. But somewhere along the way, the control I first grasped began to pull away. It became like a ghost, haunting my every move. I felt as though it was still in my hands, proving my strength and willpower. Yet, it had already slipped away into the hands of something disastrous. As much as I wanted to believe that the power was still mine, the future was out of my hands and my fate was decided.

Lent is a time to display devotion for God, but I gave my devotion to an eating disorder. Lent is a time for respect, but I started on a path of betrayal. Lent is about compassion, but I ripped apart my life and the lives of those around me. I abused its purpose. And worst of all, I began abusing myself.

Temptation

"Do you want some dessert?"

It was a simple question, but the answer would lead me through a journey of struggle and hardship.

Yes, I did want some dessert. And as I opened my mouth to say this, something took over inside of me. I heard myself saying no and as I sat watching others around me stuffing their faces with high-calorie sweets, I felt a feeling that was unfamiliar to me. It was the feeling that I was strong, that I was worth something, that I was better than others. It felt good. Much better than the usual feeling of worthlessness, I'd had for years.

The next morning when I woke up and went downstairs for breakfast, memories of the night before flooded through me like a tidal wave. I longed for that feeling to return to me, ached for it, strived for it. I stared down at the food I was about to eat. After ten minutes of staring, I finally came to a decision. The food was thrown away, never to see the inside of a stomach. Again, I felt strong. A wave of power flashed through me like a lightning bolt. I made a promise to myself to never eat breakfast again.

As long as you don't eat breakfast, I told myself, *you'll be worth something, you'll have control.*

I thought it was a good idea. But as I look back on it, I'm angry at myself for having been sucked into a tunnel of lies.

The first time I stepped on a scale and saw a number less than the time before, I felt proud. I had accomplished something that others have trouble with. I was good at something. I couldn't let that accomplishment disappear. So, when I was called down to dinner I just picked at the food. If I ate too much, the accomplishment wouldn't even matter. The hunger I felt was satisfying. It meant I had done my job. But how naïve was I to think that what I was doing was normal. That everything could just continue like it was forever. The future was inevitable. It was too late. I was beginning to become trapped, suffocated by this demon called anorexia.

Comparisons

Each person has a word that causes them to feel anger and reminds them of pain. The most common words of this kind are lies, gossip, backstabbing, fights, war, and death. Each one can be found on the top of almost anyone's "dislike list." There's no denying it. No one likes these dreadful things. I, of course, am no exception. Yet, although these words do find their way up high on my list, something much more out of the ordinary holds the number one spot.

For me, the worst word is compare. Comparing, comparer, comparison—no matter which way it's spoken, its terror beats me down all the same. And no, I'm not talking about the silly comparing that students write their essays about in school. I'm talking about something deeper, meaner. I'm talking about the comparing that rules everyday lives of competitive perfectionists like me.

It started with my brother, my baby brother. Throughout elementary school our places were clear. I was the social but serious student who always brought home report cards filled with "O's" for "outstanding." Sure, I'd get in trouble here and there, but nothing huge, just a little too chatty. My brother was different. He was a happy kid. He struggled a bit in school as the youngest in his grade. He was bursting with energy and could barely sit still long enough to learn. Constantly, his report cards read "N" for "needs improvement." It didn't mean he was bad, it just meant he had to control himself more. And that was how it was. That was who we were.

As the years passed and we both moved on to middle school, our identities began to shift. Kyle was older, more mature. He had learned self-control and started putting in full effort with school. I remained a good student, but my social life took on a more important role. Before I knew it, I earned my first C. It was in science, a subject I never fully understood. I felt like scum. Never again did I let myself receive a C. Never again would I settle for that grade. But also, never would I let myself forget about it. The C was engraved in my mind, a weapon to use against myself. Meanwhile, my brother entered middle school with straight A's. Quarter two approached and, yet again, he had straight A's. I strived to do as well as him. I strived to be as good as him. But A's with a couple of B's was the best I could do. Not only that, but as I remained in math that was a year ahead, my brother suddenly jumped up to a math that was two years ahead. It seemed as though nothing I did could compare to him. I wasn't as smart. I wasn't as studious. My little brother had slowly become better than me.

Then there were my friends. The comparisons between us were unbeatable. No matter what the comparison, I always lost. I was never as good as them. I loved them, but I hated them. They meant the world to me, but they made me cry. It wasn't their fault—it was mine. Each time I looked at them, all I saw were my own failures. They were all skinnier. They were all prettier. Most of them were smarter. Most of them were more athletic. They had better clothes. They had better lives. Everything I wasn't was everything they were. Each moment I spent with them was another moment I tore myself apart. I wanted to hang around them, but each time I felt sad. I laughed and joked with them but a part of me still felt sad. I never understood why. I never understood how. Now I understand. Now I know. The pain came from comparing myself to them. The pain always comes from comparisons.

That spring leading up to my diagnosis changed my life. Most of it happened because I compared myself to everyone else. In fact, the spark that ignited my anorexia was a series of small comparisons that banded together to create a colossal comparison of doom. It started with my brother, followed by my friends, and then ended with me tearing myself I apart.

We were in Los Angeles, at Universal Studios. It was spring break and I was sharing a hotel room with my mom, my dad, and my brother. Lent had already started and my self-imposed restrictions were still a minor part of my life. As I spent every hour around my brother, I noticed how much healthier he was eating. He ordered salads and usually skipped dessert. We were in an amusement park but he stayed away from french fries, ice cream, popcorn, and candy. Every once in a while, he ate those things, but he was careful not to over do it. My mom noticed and showered him with praise. I had noticed his healthy-eating habits back at home, but I assumed it was just a phase. But as the days passed, I realized how committed to eating healthy he truly was. Now I can assure you, his main goal wasn't to lose weight. He didn't lose weight. He just wanted to eat healthier. And he succeeded. My parents were proud. I sat there, chewing on my cotton candy, realizing how proud they were of him. I wanted them to feel that pride in me. But there I was, eating cotton candy like a fatty, while my brother snacked on an apple. I had to stop. I had to make the change just like Kyle. Not only that, but I had to do even better. He was just eating healthy; I would eat healthy and lose weight. Then, it would be clear who the healthiest eater was. I would have results. I would be the best.

Again, it only got worse with my friends. The skinniest one had gone to a doctor's appointment where she had been weighed. She confided her weight to us over lunch that May afternoon. She weighed ten pounds less than me! And she was complaining over it! She expressed the need to go on a diet. She said she would lose some weight because she was getting fat. Immediately, I began to compare. If she was getting fat, then I must already be fat. If she's fat, then I'm huge. If she's going on a diet, then I need to go on an even bigger one. From that point on, I ate less than her. If I ate less than her, than maybe I wasn't as worthless as I had thought. I needed to be better. This was the only way I could find to do that. But it didn't stop with her. Once I began comparing my food to her food, I began comparing it to everyone else's as well. My new rule was "always eat the least." It didn't matter if there were hundreds of us or just two, I could never eat more than anyone else.

As the months progressed, the tension between me and my parents reached an all-time high. For as long as I can remember, we had nasty and horrible fights. In third grade my parents even took me to a therapist to work on my anger management. Screaming matches were the usual between my mom and me. Relations with my dad weren't much better. We were both stubborn, causing us to constantly butt heads. But as my weight got lower the fights got bigger. The issue of food was just another problem to add to our list. With each fight I watched my brother with envy. He never talked back. He never got mad. My parents loved him. In their eyes he could do no wrong. But they hated me. They found flaws in me. Yet again, he was better. Yet again, I was compared and I lost.

The comparisons carried on into soccer. Every teammate I had was a competitor. If they could do one trick, I had to learn that one trick. When I couldn't, I told myself I sucked. If another girl scored a goal, I had to score a goal. When I didn't, I told myself that I had no talent. If another girl was faster, then I was a slow, lazy snail. If another girl kicked farther, then I was a weak pathetic kicker. Just as with everything else, I saw myself as the worst. I was the worst and I was nothing. The one area where I could prevail was food. The girls on my team always talked about their cravings for hamburgers or donuts. I knew that I would never want to eat a hamburger or a doughnut. At a team dinner, the girls would order appetizers. I never ate the appetizers. I felt proud. This was the only way I could be better. This was the only thing I was good at. It was another one of my dooming comparisons. It was another step in my path to destruction.

Every person, every task, every day brings a series of new comparisons. No matter whom or what or when, the comparisons always have one similarity: I'm always the loser. I'm always the one who's not good enough. I'm always the one who fails. Now you see, that is why I hate comparisons. Comparisons mess with my mind. They always lead to my self-hate and disappointment. To me, comparisons are untouchable. I try my hardest, but I never succeed. Comparisons cannot be conquered.

Beginning

It was May 2007. Memorial Day weekend was approaching and excitement was beginning to unveil itself from behind the monotonous routines of my everyday life. Our team soccer tournament at Virginia Beach was just around the corner. The crisp spring air was turning humid by the second—a fresh reminder that summer was on its way. The world seemed to be at peace. Life seemed to be as solid as ever. But that tournament, that weekend, would not arrive alone. Along with it there would be disaster. My eating disorder was about to reach a whole new level. It was about to become a tyrant. It was about to reveal itself to my family and friends.

As the car hummed along and the buildings sped past, I looked out anxiously for any sight of our hotel. It seemed as if we had been driving forever and the constant sitting was making me antsy. When we finally pulled into the hotel parking lot and I stepped out of the car, a large squeal rang through my ears, paralyzing me with shock. I regained my sanity and turned around to see three of my teammates running toward me. We giggled as we caught up and gallivanted inside, full of hope for the weekend ahead of us.

Before I knew it, morning came. The team gathered for breakfast and I faced my first of many dilemmas. I didn't eat breakfast anymore. That was the rule. No breakfast. No exceptions. It had been that way for two months now and there was absolutely no way I could forget about it. Besides, I thought, all of my friends were eating and this was my chance to show everyone I was better than them. I was stronger; I didn't need breakfast.

After breakfast, the team left to play our first game. I was in the starting lineup. The ball was kicked and the game started. The next thing I knew the world was spinning. I felt like fainting, and as I struggled to move forward, I felt as though a tunnel was enclosing me from every angle. Somewhere in the distance I heard the faint cries of encouragement from the fans. I needed to sit down. If I could just raise my hand for a sub, then that much needed rest would be mine. Trying to focus, I told myself to lift a hand into the sweltering air. But did I listen? All I could see was the ground rotating rapidly all around me. I felt myself drop. Cold water gushed down my sweaty back. I opened my eyes, unaware that I had ever closed them in the first place. I must have raised my hand because I found myself on a bench with the coach to my left and endless bottles of water to my right.

"What's wrong?" The coach asks this with worry in his voice. "We only started the game five minutes ago but you're already dead tired. Are you okay?"

Good question. Yes, that was an extremely good question. I felt as though I had been running for hours; yet, like he said, I had only just begun. I am not out of shape. Normally I can go a whole half without a sub, a whole game even. But then, there I was, only five minutes of soccer behind me, feeling as though my life was about to end. Sheer exhaustion crept onto my face. It must have been the heat. It had to be. There was no other explanation for it. Why else would I feel so dizzy and tired? That had to be it. The heat, it was all because of the heat.

After three games and two days, the tournament was beginning to come to a close. All that was left to accomplish was tackling the nearby beach with a couple of close friends. But first, our team was meeting for brunch at the Golden Corral. As soon as I heard about eating at the buffet, fear took over. Buffet—what's the first phrase that came to mind when I heard that word? All you can eat. "All you can eat" did not sound the least bit appealing to me, but for some reason my teammates eagerly awaited the food. What could I do? If I refused to go, my mom would get all pissed. She was doing that lately. I couldn't tell you why, but for some reason she was starting to get pretty uptight about food. So I went. I mustered up my courage, walked into the buffet, and grabbed myself a plate. An hour later I sat staring into the distance, overwhelmed with guilt. Sure, everyone else had gone back for seconds, even thirds, while I just halfway filled up my first plate. But that didn't matter because I had eaten five french fries. Did you hear me!? French fries! Five of them! *Wow*, I thought, *I'm horrible. I have no self-control and I'm going to become fat now. I officially suck.*

As soon as the others were done stuffing their faces, we headed off to the beach. Once there, we all lay down on our towels and lathered up with suntan lotion. This was supposed to be fun and relaxing. Isn't that what tanning on a beach with your friends is all about? However, all I felt was despair. I had eaten five french fries and now what was I doing? I was just lying there like a lazy, old cow. I had to get moving. It was the only way to burn off those french fries and regain my pride. So I convinced some girls to go shopping along the boardwalk with me. As we laughed and talked our way down the beach, I found my mind constantly turning back to the french fries. It was like an endless Ferris wheel, pulling me away from the happiness and joy that so clearly shone on my friends' faces. The sun was bright above us, yet all I saw were clouds. The large cloud I felt hovering above me seemed to wash my happiness into the vast ocean.

My friends decided to stop for ice cream. Mmmm, ice cream. It sounded so good, and my stomach growled with hunger as the word floated out of my mouth into the air.

All the more reason not to eat any, I thought. *Don't give in to the temptation. Regain your strength. You already ate like a fatty today, don't let that happen again.*

So that was that. No ice cream for me. And although I craved the cold, gooey chocolate as it dripped from the flaky cones my friends held, the power of resisting it tasted sweet inside my mouth. To me, the taste of power was much better than any food in the world. And I had no doubt—I would do whatever I could to hold on to that taste for as long as possible.

On the ride home, I opened my eyes just in time to witness my dad turn off the road and drive the car into an empty parking lot. I looked around with curiosity, wondering where we were. As I looked at the sign in the distance, I felt dread inch its way into my thoughts. We were at Cracker Barrel. Yet again, it was time to eat. Looking around at my family filled me with a hollow sadness. They were "starving" and impatiently waiting to eat. It was unfair, I realized. They got to look forward to eating, they got to be hungry. I remember when I felt like that. But lately, the only emotions food had given me were guilt and dread. For a moment, I wondered why. But I quickly brushed the thought out of my mind, assured that deep down they felt guilt and dread too. And that was the answer. They all felt like me, they just never showed it. See, I'm completely normal!

Once we were seated, the tension started to rise. Considering that I'm vegetarian, we all agreed my best option would be the "three sides" combo. But which sides to choose was the real issue. Of course, I just wanted veggies. It was an easy choice. Corn, green beans, and carrots were what I would order. But my mom had other plans.

"Vegetables are not a meal. You WILL get another food group. Have some mashed potatoes. Or better yet, get macaroni and cheese!" She wasn't suggesting this. It was a demand. And by the pure fire I saw in her eyes, I could tell she meant business. However, I was determined too. I went along and ordered some mashed potatoes, but I made an exaggerated point of just picking at them hoping that would show my mom who was boss. I had control.

It was the first of many arguments our family would have over meals. It was the start of an ongoing battle between my mom and me. For her, it was the beginning of a realization. For me, it was the beginning of a power struggle. But no matter which way you choose to look at it, that dinner was a beginning.

Beauty

Beauty. What does that word mean? We hear it everywhere we go. It's coolly dropped into every conversation. Everything you do, everything you say, somehow brings you back to that word. It's such a phenomenon in our society. It always has been and unfortunately, my guess is, it always will be. Each person has her own definition of the word. Each person has her own reason for wanting to achieve it.

There's the diligent student. The girl who spends so much time studying that she has no time for fashion or friends. This girl always has a book in her hand and a frown on her face. She is cast aside from the crowd and doesn't fit in. At times she feels happy, but the majority of her life she spends feeling alone. To her, beauty is the ticket to popularity. If only she were beautiful, she would have more friends. If only she were beautiful, she would be on the inside looking out, instead of on the outside looking in. She would be popular.

But the popular girl strives for beauty too. To her, beauty is a necessity. If she slips up and loses her beauty, her world might come tumbling down. She is pressured to always look her best. She can never leave her house without makeup, and she must always dress to impress. A bad hair day is unacceptable. Beauty defines her identity and she can't afford to lose it.

Then there is the girl dressed in all black. Her hair always goes unbrushed, and she wears chains all over. To this girl beauty is a struggle. She feels as though it can never be reached. Realizing this, she tries to hide her flaws. Instead of striving for beauty, she does everything she can to avoid it. Maybe, if it looks like she doesn't care about beauty, people won't care that she doesn't have any.

And some people view beauty as out of their control. So, in an attempt to change this, they work on the only thing they know how to control—their weight. With each pound they lose, the more beautiful they feel. Those girls strive to be skinny because to them skinny equals beauty. Yet, as they get skinnier and skinnier they slowly drift farther away from whatever beauty they once had. And at the end of the day, no matter how much weight they lost, they still don't feel beautiful. So they continue on their quest for beauty by forcing themselves to become even skinnier.

Personally, I can relate to all of these girls. I constantly wonder what would happen if I looked prettier. Would more people like me? Would I like myself? I, too, feel as though I can't leave the house without makeup. I always attempt to wear the cutest outfits. And then there are times when I try to go unnoticed, hoping that no one will see me the way I see myself. And every day I feel as though if I stay skinny I can feel pretty. But it never works out that way.

Beauty is unattainable—at least in the way I view it. To me, beauty is perfection. Our society drills it into our heads that beauty is power. The prettier you are, the better you are, the more guys you get. But perfection does not exist. Nothing is perfect. Every person has flaws. Every life has struggles. Every success has failures. Behind every truth there are lies. And behind each strength, there is a weakness. Beauty is not possible.

Yet, many girls hurt themselves trying to achieve it. They develop eating disorders or get plastic surgery. They turn their backs on their friends or change their identity. But real beauty shines within those flaws. Real beauty emerges through the problems and the lies. Real beauty is achieved when you can find it within yourself.

Innocence

Innocence: (noun) lack of knowledge or understanding
Naïve: (adjective) showing a lack of experience, judgment, or information

Thinking back on life near the end of eighth grade, these are the only words that come to mind. They pretty much sum up who I was then and what I knew of the world.

Since that April, my mom casually made comments about my weight here and there. Nothing huge, just a subtle, "you look a little skinnier" or "those pants are looking a little loose." But it wasn't until late May that the comments morphed into serious demands. The transformation was clear. There was no mistaking the desperate cries of "you really need to eat more" or "don't get up from the table unless you finish that."

As early June came rolling in, my mom took action. She had been threatening to take me to my pediatrician for weeks but I had somehow wriggled out of it every time. That is—until the last day of school. It was my last day of middle school, the beginning of my high school journey, and the beginning of a more independent lifestyle. Little did I know high school wasn't the only journey I was about to take. Recovery was just around the corner and facing that would be harder than anything else I had ever faced. It would shrink me into the darkness multiple times. Then it would watch as I burst back into the light, striking it to the ground with success. And it all started with the first doctor's appointment. It started in third period. It started with a note.

I was halfway through the boring drones of my history teacher when the note came. I looked at it with hope because we all knew that notes from the office led to early dismissal. Excitedly, I turned the note over and read its unknown black ink. Underneath the title "Reason" was a little box with a check next to doctor's appointment.

Suddenly I felt enclosed by the walls around me. The secrets, the future, the lies, all began to swirl around me like a bottomless vortex. I gasped for breath. *NO*, I thought, *NO, NO! I can't go there. They will weigh me. They will see how much I've lost.*

To me the weight loss was perfectly fine. In fact, it was something to be proud of, something to cherish. And of course, I already knew how much I weighed since I had recently started weighing myself three to five times a day. It wasn't what I weighed that scared me. It was the thought that what I weighed would be revealed. Sure, it may have meant success to me, but something told me my mom wouldn't see it the same way. She had openly and clearly expressed her desire for me to gain weight. I knew the doctor would back her up. And at that moment, in that mind set, on that day, weight gain was NOT an option.

I desperately went to "plan A." As usual, I had skipped breakfast and only ate an apple for lunch. So the second I scurried into the lunch room and found my way through the mass of people scrambling for their place, I ran to my friends and watched in awe as the lies began to spiral out of my mouth.

"Oh my god guys! I forgot my lunch! Ah, I'm so ditzy; it was on the table right next to the door." I had no idea where these words were coming from but the fact that everyone was staring right at me gave me the idea that they came directly from my own mouth.

"Please, if you guys have anything extra would you mind giving it to me? I'm starving!" They seemed shocked. At the time I had no clue why, but to tell you the truth, I really didn't care. All that mattered was for them to listen, so I sat back and waited. I didn't have to wait long because they quickly began hurling leftovers, cookies, and other snacks my way. I showered them with thanks and inspected the assortment of food in front of me. I selected three of the items and began to eat. Finishing right as the bell rang, I reflected in satisfaction. I felt certain that eating those three things would put me at a good weight. I was certain my mom would be satisfied. I was certain it would all be okay, and tomorrow I would return to my new eating habits. Tomorrow life would go on.

But just to make sure, I turned to "plan B." I asked my math teacher if she had a phone I could borrow. I told her there was an "emergency" and overwhelmed her with gratitude as she showed me the staff phone in the next room. I rapidly dialed my mom's cell and once again, the lies began to unravel.

I pleaded with her, begged her, and attempted to bribe her. I tried anything and everything to get out of that doctor's appointment. I heard myself build up a story with increasing speed. I was telling her how badly I wanted to stay in school. Taking me out early on the last day would mean missing out on all the good-byes. I heard myself crying. CRYING! And it was all over one little doctor's appointment. At that moment I probably should've have realized something was off. It's not like every teenager would cry over leaving school early. It's not like every teenager would feel a desperate need to keep her weight a secret. But I was not like every teenager. Yet, somehow, I hadn't realized this yet. Somehow, I thought I was normal. I thought life was going great. I thought that this doctor's appointment was completely unnecessary, completely absurd.

Needless to say, my attempts to escape didn't work that time. And that doctor's appointment was the first in an ongoing series. A long line of other appointments soon followed.

Irony

My eighth grade English teacher told us about the assignment. It was the same assignment given every year to every eighth grade student. Our teacher told us to write a reflection on our years at the middle school. We needed to include what had changed and what we had learned—these were the only guidelines. The catch was that two reflections from each English teacher would be chosen, and those students would be brought in to privately read their speech to the team of staff members. In the end, only two people in the whole grade of about 350 students would be chosen to read their reflection at graduation. They would stand on a podium in front of the whole grade and all the parents. Most kids were dying to be picked. But to me, the reward sounded too embarrassing. I didn't think much about the assignment over the next month because it wasn't that important to me. Besides, there was no way they would ever pick me. I was much more interested in food and exercise those days anyways. I don't think I even started the essay until the night before it was due. My mom always said I was a procrastinator. But from the moment I sat down and began to type, I could feel the words just flowing out of me. I didn't even reread the final product; I just typed it up in half an hour and turned it in the following day.

Two weeks later, my teacher told us she had made her decision. When she added that one of her chosen students was in our class period, I witnessed my classmates around me sit up in anticipation. Then my name was called out. I heard her say it but it didn't feel real. I just sat there as everyone in the room began to clap. My friend pats me on the back and urged me to stand up. I was sure I had heard wrong. I put minimal effort into the essay, but I had felt like it was one of my better pieces of work. But being chosen? That just sounded too absurd to be true. I wasn't good at anything. I wasn't special. I wasn't worthy. Or at least, that's what I constantly lead myself to believe. Although I said I didn't care about it, I felt a surge of excitement at the realization that I was picked. Secretly, I had hoped for it. Secretly, I needed it.

All of the finalists were asked in to read their speeches the following week. As I sat listening to the cleverly crafted reflections of my peers, I felt positive that I would never win. Each speech seemed better than the last and mine didn't even compare. That's how I saw it, but I was wrong. Finding out that the panel had chosen me as one of the two finalists was surreal to say the least. Somebody actually thought I was good at something. The thought shocked me but filled me with unusual pride. But it was almost unbelievable pride. It was like I knew I should be feeling proud because I had succeeded, but at the same time, there was this little voice inside, telling me the accomplishment was just a fluke. This little voice inside me said I was still the worthless piece of crap I always had been. That voice told me that if I wanted to be proud, I had to prove that I deserved it. And the only way I could think of doing so was by not eating. That week I grew even stricter about my meals. I pushed myself to lose weight so that I could feel like the reward was well earned. Why I thought weight loss signified that I deserved to be chosen was beyond me.

As graduation grew closer, my eating habits worsened. I was scared. I was scared of being laughed at. I was scared of looking stupid. My speech was extremely personal and sharing it with each one of my classmates seemed mortifying. I was certain they would all hate it. I was certain they'd all make fun of me behind my back. With each new set of nerves, I began to eat less and less. It was the first, but definitely not the last, time that my eating disorder got extremely out of hand. I didn't eat anything the day of the performance. But somehow, that seemed all right. I told myself it was just because of the nerves. I convinced myself that I was just too nervous to eat. And when my stomach began to ache an hour before I was to read the speech, again I blamed it on my nerves.

The shining lights blinded me as I stepped onto the stage and looked out at the auditorium in front of me. I couldn't pick out faces, but I knew who was out there. I knew my friends were watching with excitement. I knew the boys that constantly teased me were staring up with smirks on their faces. I knew that somewhere toward the back my parents were watching, trying not to cry. I tried to push these images out of my mind. I took a deep breath and began to say my speech. It went like this:

"Two roads diverged in a wood, I took the one less traveled by and that has made all the difference." This is a quote from "The Road Less Traveled" by Robert Frost, the man after whom our school is named. There have been many times that I have read a poem and had no idea what it meant, but this particular poem is different. As I read the words written by this man, not only can I understand what he is saying but I find myself relating it to my life. Throughout the past three years there have been many instances when I have had a choice to make. In some cases, I would find that I was weak and I would go along with the crowd. However, there were times when I took a chance and chose "the road less traveled by." I find that as my life as a Frost student continues, I chose "the road less traveled by," more and more. I feel that one important lesson I have learned during middle school is that it is okay to be different. We are teenagers—most of us thirteen- or fourteen-years-old. Every day we feel the pressure to fit in. Nobody wants to be the loser or the outcast. Nobody wants to be alone with no friends. So we find ourselves, or at least I do, going along with the crowd and taking the more traveled on road. But as I grow older, I have begun to learn that I don't have to take that road. Sometimes taking a chance and being different is better. That is a lesson that I know I will take with me into high school and that I will remember forever. Not only has my journey at Frost taught me important lessons such as that but it has changed me as a person. When I entered the school in sixth grade, I was timid and scared. I didn't know many people. I stayed to myself and put all my attention into schoolwork. As I got older and went on to seventh and eighth grade, I became much more outgoing. I let myself meet new people and make new friendships. When I think of all the friendships I have made in the past three years I know that I have made a few that will last my whole life. I don't know if I could've made it through the middle school years without my friends by my side and I know they will help me get through high school too. If someone were to ask me right now what I think of Frost, it would be hard to answer. To be honest, I'm a teenager and it's a school so I wouldn't be able to say that it's the most amazing place in the world. However, I would be able to say that it's a place where I feel safe and a place that I will definitely miss as I go on to Wootton. I am thankful that I was able to go to such a good school with such great teachers. I think that because of the lessons I learned at Frost I will be much more successful in high school. Robert Frost Middle School gave me many good memories that I will never forget. I won't forget the teachers who have tried to prepare me for high school. I won't forget the hours I've put into homework and studying for tests. I won't forget the times I've wished I could just crawl into a hole for the rest of the day. I won't forget the first day of sixth grade when I walked into the lunchroom and saw the faces of what seemed like a thousand strangers. I was scared out of my mind when I saw all those people who I had never met. Little did I know that three years later I would call them my friends. And now, as I'm getting ready for high school, I'm starting to get scared all over again. The difference is this time I know everything will be okay.

As I finished off the speech I blew out a sign of relief. My legs were still trembling and my palms were still sweaty. But I couldn't stop myself from smiling when the whole crowd burst into cheers. I was embarrassed, but proud. I was scared, but confident. I was seemingly mature, but in reality, I was clueless. As I spoke these words I had no idea of what was to come. As I spoke these words I had no idea that I was already becoming suffocated by anorexia. I had no idea I was already in the eating disorder's grasp. I was clueless and I thought that my life was perfect. I even treated myself to an Italian ice after the graduation because I felt so optimistic. Obviously, I should've known something was up when the first food I ate all day was an Italian ice and even that made me feel immersed in guilt. But like I said, I was clueless.

So much of that speech was a lie. It's not that I meant to lie. It's just that I believed those lies, my own lies. I was tricked into thinking this way in my eating disorder's attempt to divert me from the real problem. None of what I depicted reflected how I really felt. None of what I predicted would come true. Nothing I said would become reality.

"In some cases, I would find that I was weak and I would go along with the crowd. However, there were times when I took a chance and chose 'the road less traveled by.'"

When I started my speech off with this thought, I meant it to be positive. But the different "road" I ended up taking led to dangerous hardships. And in reality, I didn't choose the different road to find myself; I chose that different road in an attempt to accept myself. In an odd way, I became different because I wanted to be the same. I became anorexic because I wanted to be better. I pushed myself to be skinny because I wanted to be beautiful. I pushed myself to resist food because I wanted to be powerful. Yes, I did choose a different road; however, I chose it for all the wrong reasons.

"But as I grow older, I have begun to learn that I don't have to take that road. Sometimes taking a chance and being different is better."

This part of the speech was supposed to be true. As I wrote it, I knew it sounded like a good lesson and that it was probably a lesson I should've learned. So I wrote about it as if it were real. But in the meantime, I was trying desperately to fit in. I felt like everyone around me was better in some way and I wanted that to change. I wanted to feel as good as everyone else. I wanted to feel like I wasn't scum. I didn't want to feel worthless anymore. I said that this was a lesson I had learned, but really, being different sounded more unappealing than ever.

"When I entered the school in sixth grade, I was timid and scared. I didn't know many people. I stayed to myself and put all my attention into schoolwork. As I got older and went on to seventh and eighth grade, I became much more outgoing."

As these lines of the reflection were written, I believed that they were real. I felt more outgoing. I felt less timid. Or at least, that's how I acted. I was loud and talkative. I had plenty of friends. I put on a smile when I really felt pain, and I laughed when all I wanted to do was cry. So saying that I was outgoing didn't seem unrealistic. I knew people would believe it without question. But deep down, I was even more timid and scared than sixth grade and the outgoing personality was just a cover-up. In reality, I was suffering from low self-esteem. In reality, I hated myself. In reality, I was miserable.

"When I think of all the friendships I have made in the past three years I know that I have made a few that will last my whole life. I don't know if I could've made it through the middle school years without my friends by my side and I know they will help me get through high school too."

At the time that I wrote that, I actually believed it. I felt as though I had the world's most supportive friends. I felt as though nothing could tear us apart. This is how I saw our friendship. But in the months to come, I would find that I was completely wrong. Aside from Meredith, none of my friends were there when I needed them the most. None of them would remain my friends for even another year. None of them would stay by my side or help me get through high school. Yet another fine example of how clueless I really was.

"And now, as I'm getting ready for high school, I'm starting to get scared all over again. The difference is this time I know everything will be okay."

My closing statement turned out to be the most false of them all. This line was an optimistic end to a happy and positive speech. But it couldn't be further from the truth. My fear of high school could never be worse than the reality. My freshman year was about to become a nightmare. I was about to be sucked into a destructive tornado. I was about to be shrunken away until I was near death. I was about to have to fight to survive and endure months of physical and emotional pain. I was about to be betrayed and cheated on and gossiped about. "Everything will be okay," I said. Yeah right.

Lies

It had been a month since that first doctor's appointment. A month since my mom had begun taking action. I sat there silently listening to the doctor drone on about how important a healthy diet is and all the usual crap. *Yeah, Yeah, Yeah*, I thought to myself as her tone turned serious, *I already have a healthy diet so you can stop wasting your time lady*. In fact, when I thought about it, I have one of the healthiest diets of anyone I know. I mean I never eat sweets or drink soda. I always have an apple for lunch. I never eat junky cereal considering I never eat breakfast. Oh, and I never go back for seconds at dinner. In fact, sometimes I don't even finish my firsts. Yeah, I'm healthy for sure. Thinking this, I let the doctor go on with her nonsense as I felt a wave of satisfaction wash over me.

"…and then the dietician can help you with your diet. You should try to see her within the next week or so…" The doctor's words hit me like a brick. What was she talking about? What dietician? Oh god, I really should pay attention more.

The next week I discovered what she meant. An appointment had been set up with a dietician and my vital signs were quickly taken as we shuffled into her clustered office. Protein—that word seemed to be all she could say. Apparently, as a vegetarian I wasn't getting the much-needed protein that's found in meat. She went on and on about how to get more protein and how much I need in a day. Somewhere in her long, pointless speech I heard the word ninety.

"I'm sorry, what was that?" I asked with caution, scared to hear the answer.

"Ninety," she repeated. "You should have ninety grams of protein every day."

Now that does it. At the moment I was completely and utterly convinced that this lady was a psycho. Obviously, she wanted me to do the impossible. Nobody had that much protein in one day. She wanted me to be fat. I definitely was not going to listen to anything she said.

However, along with her insane suggestions came one appealing idea. She wanted me to keep a food journal. Each time I ate or drank something I was supposed to write it down in the journal. Then, each time I visited her, I would show her what I had been doing since we last met. This was perfect. Up until then, I added up everything I ate during the day before I could fall asleep at night. If I didn't rehash the foods of the day, I couldn't sleep. It was that simple. And now I had an easier way to keep track.

I soon learned that the food journal wouldn't turn out the way I had planned. Each date had multiple lines to put multiple foods on. Yet, as I filled out the food I ate on that first day, I realized how many lines I left empty. The dietician had told me to fill up the whole page, but I was only filling up the first two or three lines. *Wow*, I said to myself, *this lady is crazier than I thought*

I had to lie. It wasn't like I wanted to or anything. It's just the grownups were leaving me with no other option. For some odd reason they didn't appreciate my new healthy diet and wanted me to eat way more than any normal person would. They were conspiring against me. So you see, I had to lie. I had to. But I soon found—even with the made-up foods I added to my list—I still didn't impress the adults. I thought the list was huge. With the amounts of food I put down I was sure they'd be satisfied. But their disapproval only encouraged me more. Lies became bigger. Truths became smaller. My feeling of loneliness expanded along with time.

Tricks began to pop into my mind. Ways to convince became ideas ready to be tested. I snuck downstairs one afternoon and slyly opened the top right drawer. I locked my hand around a plastic bag, jerked it back out, and rapidly ran up the stairs, clinging on to the bag as I went. Once in the safe haven of my room, I put the bag underneath my bed and breathed a sign of relief. Plan number one of my sinful life was underway. As the days passed, the bag filled up along with the lies I told.

They wanted me to eat a protein bar. Okay fine, I take it upstairs, rip open the wrapper and stuff the bar in the bag. I proudly waltz back down the stairs, swinging the empty wrapper for the world to see. My mom looks up and we make eye contact. I smile as she glances at my hand. The realization that it's empty strikes her and she looks away with hope. At this point I know I should feel guilt. But oddly, all I feel is pride. Success is mine. I have tricked my mom. I was tricking the doctor. I will trick the dietician. Supposedly, grown-ups were wiser, with more knowledge of the world than naïve little children. Yet, here I was putting one over on them all.

It became a regular occurrence. Every day was filled with more and more lies. Each appointment with the doctor, each meeting with the dietician, each argument with my mom all had one thing in common: the pressure for me to eat more. And with each one, I willingly agreed, secretly knowing that every word I spoke was just another story. And that's exactly what they were. They were stories. Every time guilt began to appear, I shrugged it off. I wasn't a liar. I was just a storyteller. And I had to tell these stories. It was for my own good. I was right and everyone else was wrong. Back then it was me against the world. That was how I liked it—me against the world.

Oblivious

Describing the summer leading up to my diagnosis is difficult. It depends on which perspective you look at it. To me, that summer was blissful and carefree. I felt strong and on top of the world, as I continuously restricted foods while watching others around me give in to the temptations. But to those around me I was becoming weaker with each day. They watched with angst as I slowly lost myself to a devastating disease.

That summer I landed myself a job as a counselor in training at a kid's day camp. I didn't get paid, but the six weeks of work provided me with all the community service hours I needed to graduate. The job was tiring and required every ounce of energy I had. I constantly chased after kids, broke up fights, and provided entertainment through games such as tag, dodge ball, and soccer. Unfortunately for me, I continued to lose more and more energy as I was rapidly sucked into oblivion.

The weekend before camp started all the staff had to attend a mandatory meeting. We assembled in our designated classrooms to set up and brainstorm for the long six weeks ahead of us. As we vigorously scrubbed the colorful desks (which we soon found were not meant to be colorful), an anxious feeling began to rise up through my veins and take over my soul. It was the feeling that I would become fat. It was the feeling that this summer would ruin all the hard work I had previously put into losing weight.

The feeling arose as I listened to the veteran counselors enlighten us from their past experiences.

"Oh god, the problem with working here is the food."

"I know! There are always so many sweets lying around. I swear, each year I gain at least five pounds."

They went on to talk about the delicious staff lunches that appeared once every week, the endless amounts of chocolate lying around the kitchen, the daily doughnuts brought in for breakfast, and the constant munching on the children's snacks.

Well they may gain weight while working here, but not me! I thought this with determination and courage. I would be better. I would be stronger. I would not let myself follow in the others' footsteps. In fact, I would lose weight while they gained it. Yes, that was it. That was what I would do. And just like that it was decided. It was now my goal and nothing could stop me from reaching it.

The first test of achieving this goal arrived on the first day of camp. Just as I had expected, I walked into the main office only to find boxes and boxes of Dunkin' Donuts. There were rows and rows of hot, doughy, sugary pastries and a huge group of people surrounding them. They were like vultures waiting to attack their prey. I made a sharp turn and scurried over to the bathroom on the opposite side of the hall. I locked myself in one of the stalls and gave myself an internal pep talk.

If you eat even one bite of a doughnut you are a bad person. You will become fat. Don't you remember, you weighed yourself this morning and were a pound less than you were two days ago? Now think about it, no matter how delicious the food, nothing is worth ruining that achievement.

So that was that. I left the bathroom and walked directly past the doughnuts and into the classroom. A sense of pride rushed through me and a smile crept onto my face.

As I think back, it amazes me how blind I was in such an obvious moment of deception. Any sane person would have realized that this thought process was absurd. One bite of anything, no matter how sugary or fattening, can't make you fat. And to enjoy something sweet does not make you a bad person—it just makes you human.

But that was the problem; I wasn't sane. The common sense and truth that once existed no longer mattered because my mind had been abducted by a conniving eating disorder. This eating disorder would continue to interrupt my life. It had an impact as it hid behind the lies I told myself. But the impact would only worsen in time as the truth began to unwind.

Yes, to me that summer is hard to explain. My view on it differs completely from what all of the others around me witnessed. Yet no matter which way you look at it, there is no denying that it was the summer that changed my life.

Work

The people I worked with started to act like my mother. I had been working at the summer camp for two weeks and I had three more to go. With each passing day my co-counselors grew more and more suspicious. I sat there every morning watching them munch on the doughnuts, and they retaliated by watching me munch on air. I told them I ate breakfast before I came. It was just a little white lie. No harm in that. *Besides,* I would explain to myself, *they're older; they just don't understand how life is these days. No one eats breakfast anymore. It's not like I'm the only one.*

They accepted my morning lies, but the lunches proved more difficult to get around. Constantly the others would raise an eyebrow at my miniscule lunch. They asked me with shock if all I had to eat was an apple. I assured them I had already eaten a sandwich while they were focusing on trouble-making kids. They nodded their heads and changed the subject, but something in their voices told me they weren't easy to fool. The first few weeks went on like this. More raised eyebrows along with more lying. Eventually they stopped. What could they do? They had just met me and it wasn't their place to confront me about my eating habits. I knew that. They knew that. So much was left unsaid while we went along with the motions of each tedious day.

The trouble was the kids. They all adored me. The girls fought over who could hold my hand; and, the boys talked for hours, telling me about their pet dog or new toy. They watched my every move. I was a fool for thinking they wouldn't notice my lack of lunch.

"Nicole," one girl said as she stared up at me, wide-eyed with a toothy grin, "I want to be like you. That's why I brought this apple today instead of my cookies."

I quickly discouraged her, telling her it was good to enjoy her cookies and her apples too. Why did she need to pick one? Luckily, she listened, and returned the next day with both an apple and an assortment of cookies. She offered me one and wouldn't accept no for an answer. As I nibbled on the crunchy chocolate flakes I decided there was no way I could eat my apple after that. I threw it away without question.

Looking back, I wonder how I didn't see it. Why could I recognize that that sweet, little girl could eat both foods but I wouldn't let myself have the same option? Why couldn't I realize that I needed to start taking my own advice?

Unfortunately, at the time, none of it clicked. I still was oblivious to the problem, obeying each command my anorexia made without question. That proved true each Thursday morning at out staff meetings. They were held in a little room attached to the main office. We gathered there in the confined space that held one long table and six chairs as our campers goofed around in the pool. We discussed what we needed to work on and what we were doing well. But of course, I missed out on the majority of the discussion, preoccupied with my new obsession—food.

A treat was provided at each meeting. Some weeks we had popsicles, other times bagels, and sometimes we were offered bowls of miniature chocolates or small brownie bites. The counselors anticipated the meetings for that reason and that reason only. I anticipated those foods too, even though I rarely allowed myself to eat them. I looked forward to discovering which food would be provided that week and which counselors would choose to eat some. I had a blast, sitting there and watching how each person ate and how much. I began to feel like observing others eating was the most enjoyable pastime in the world. Don't ask me why; I couldn't tell you. All I know is that was how it was. That was what my life had become. Sitting there happy as my stomach growled its hunger and those around me filling up on harmful sweets.

One time I decided to be daring. I had another one of those pointless doctor's appointments directly after attending the meeting. I knew it was coming and knew they would weigh me. I thought back on the past few days, reminiscing on all I ate. I thought that I had done a good job. But it seemed as if each success in my book was a failure in my mom's. I had to do something to spike the number up on that scale, and fast.

The treat of the week was bagels. We sat down, squished between one another, fighting for a place as the tray appeared in front of us. They smelled fresh, evident by the steam making its way up to the ceiling. Every kind of cream cheese imaginable surrounded the tray, and the staff around me seemed like a pack of wolves. They were carefully waiting for the right moment to dig into the glorious pile.

"Dig in!" The leader cried, barely spitting her words out before hands and bagels began to fly everywhere. I waited tentatively, battling myself on what to do. As the chaos subsided, I made up my mind. I reached out my hand, watching it shake as it took hold of the bagel. I had a deep feeling that I would regret this. But I slowly smeared the light cream cheese on in the thinnest layer I could and began to eat. Half way through the bagel, I was certain I had gained at least two pounds. I declared myself done as I tried not to cry from the immense amount of guilt arising from my sin. But I was certain I had succeeded in my goal. I knew this bagel would make me gain weight. And I knew a weight gain would get my mom off my case and convince everyone I was fine. Because I was fine, I was sure of it. And now, because of the sacrifice I made by eating half of a bagel, everyone else would be sure of it too.

I was wrong. Way wrong. Somehow, I had lost weight when I found myself stepping on the scale that same Thursday afternoon. Somehow, the bagel hadn't done its job. My mom was not satisfied and she most definitely did not get off my case. For a second, I wondered why my plan failed. But I was quickly reassured by a voice in my head. It was all just a fluke. The scale was messed up. You ate a bagel, now you're fat. Bad idea, because now you're going to have to pay.

Saving Up

Macaroni Grill. Hearing the name hadn't scared me for years. Back when I was about five-years-old we tried to eat at Macaroni Grill but had to leave before getting served. There was a vast opening that allowed customers to see into the kitchen. The opening displayed a tremendous fire pit for cooking. I was in the "ah, it's fire!" stage and immediately began to cry at the sight of the pit.

But times were different now; I was older and braver, way past that stage of my life. I grew to love Macaroni Grill and, up until becoming vegetarian, I indulged myself in their hearty lasagna and gobbled up their beef ravioli. So when my parents suggested going there for dinner the next Friday night, I was utterly surprised to find myself scared. I knew it wasn't the fire that scared me. We had gone many times since I was little and I had been fine. But on that steamy July day I found myself shaken at the thought of eating at the well-known Italian restaurant. I tried to convince my parents to pick someplace else.

"Can we not go to an Italian restaurant? Please. That's the last type of food I feel like eating right now," I declared as the day of the outing arrived.

"But honey," my parents responded, "you love Italian food. And so does the rest of the family." So there you have it. The decision was made and there was nothing I could do but prepare myself for the meal to come.

That day I drilled myself hard. If I wanted to enjoy the food, I had to save up some calories. I knew the number of calories of every meal at that restaurant, just like I knew the calorie count of items at every other restaurant, and I can assure you that one meal there would equal three days' worth of food for me. But I wanted to enjoy it. I wanted to taste the yummy, cheesy pasta. Okay, so maybe I wouldn't order anything too cheesy. That's a lot of fat after all. But I could get plain spaghetti with tomato sauce, and if I felt extra rebellious I might even sprinkle on a little Parmesan cheese.

But to eat all that—I had to earn it. I took extra precautions the day before the big dinner. Each food I consumed had to be one hundred calories or less. No fats. No carbs. The following day was even worse. I silenced my hunger time and time again as I ordered myself not to eat at all. Obviously, I didn't need to eat; I would get a day's worth of food and more at dinner that night. It was just an opportunity to show some self-control. I disciplined myself to be patient. I disciplined myself to stay strong.

By the time we pulled into the parking lot my stomach was pleading for food. I was starving, yet somehow the hunger felt satisfying. After all, it was a sign I had done a good job. It was a sign I had more control than food. The satisfaction stole the attention from the sharp pains I was feeling in my stomach. *Besides,* I told myself, *you deserve the pain.* I repeated this to myself continuously as we were escorted to our seats right next to my old friend "the fire pit."

I ordered without hesitation. While everyone else skimmed the menu desperately trying to make a choice, I shut the menu, pushed it aside, and happily folded my hands in my lap. I had made my decision a week in advance. I had come prepared unlike the clueless people surrounding me. Their decisions wavered from one food to the next while I sat there sure. I was sure of myself and sure of the food. Just another sign at how in control I was. I was proud. I couldn't let the pride disappear.

The food was laid in front of me. I stared at it as though it were a person with a gun. Fear radiated out of me and doubt spread across my face. I watched as my family dove in, trying to picture myself doing the same. Until then I had felt as though I was on top of the world. I had put so much effort into the past two days and was rewarded with the success of extreme hunger. Up until that point I had done everything right. But if I ate the meal, if I followed through with my plan, all the hard work would mean nothing. My pride would be flushed away with shame. My satisfaction would be kicked to the side, watching as guilt took center stage. Eating that spaghetti would ruin everything. I just couldn't do it. So what, I'd enjoy it for ten minutes? That wasn't worth it. Nothing was worth it. Only a fool would choose to feel shame and guilt over pride and satisfaction. And I was not a fool. I wouldn't be. I couldn't be.

I picked up a fork and began to twiddle it around the long noodles. The sauce dripped like soup as I lifted up a chunk of it with my spoon. I squished down on the tomato pieces and slowly mixed the sauce into the noodles. The yellow pasta turned a deep red as it soaked in the sauce. I grabbed a knife and began to work. I cut it up horizontally, then vertically, then horizontally and so on until the long noodles became tiny clumps. I put a bite in my mouth and then began to twirl, squish, and cut some more. Another bite and more twirling began. Before I knew it, the plates around me were polished clean. My family looked stuffed. I had a huge heap of spaghetti still remaining on my plate, and I was fully aware that I had eaten only a small portion of the food. Yet, I somehow felt full too. My stomach was bloated. I felt like a balloon that was expanding by the minute. I had eaten no more than ten bites in an attempt to maintain the pride I had felt so recently. But even that was not good enough. Eating that small amount of food filled me with shame. I hated myself. I hated myself and I hated food. I hated what it did to me and what it didn't. I hated who I was and who I was starting to become. Although I wasn't aware of it, I was changing. Each battle with food became another victory for my life-destroying foe. I had no clue I was in a fight but it didn't matter. My eating disorder was kicking my butt and nothing was going to stop it.

Symptoms

Chills swivel their way up my spine. My hands are tinted blue from the cold. My teeth chatter uncontrollably and my legs begin to shiver. I'm in a blizzard. Snow dances around me with intensity. My shoulders feel weighed down from the many layers of clothing I have piled on. All I can hear are the streaks of wind blazing past my ears. I can barely move, paralyzed by the frigid weather that surrounds me.

Desperately, I open my eyes to see where I am. Confusion develops as I stare straight into the blistering sun above my head. I'm shaken out of my vision, reality crashing down on me. It's not winter at all. There is no blizzard. In fact, it's mid-August and the temperature outside is nearing one hundred degrees. I look around and am surrounded by panting people in tank tops, shorts, and sandals. They look worn down from the heat. Sweat drips from their agonized faces.

And then I look down at myself. My legs are still shivering and my teeth are still chattering. I wear sweatpants and a sweatshirt, yet I still feel those chills traveling up my spine. I roll up my sleeve and look at my arm. Goosebumps appear in scattered places while my hands still look blue from being cold. Its summer but I still feel like I'm back in the blizzard. I still feel like a frozen chunk of ice.

Sadly, this was not unusual for me. It seemed cold was the common feeling I had lately. It hadn't always been this way though. I used to be one of those sweaty people burning up from the summer heat. I used to be one of those people yearning for a nice pool to jump in or a cool ice cream bar to eat. But for some unknown reason, this summer was different. No way would I ever yearn for that ice cream again. For one, I was already freezing, no matter how hot the weather was. For another, ice cream is a "bad" food. I simply couldn't eat it, at least not if I wanted to stay skinny.

Skinny—the word was beginning to interfere with my life and take over my thoughts. It was the main reason I had trouble sleeping each night. I used to be a sound sleeper. Since about sixth grade, I had cherished sleep and gotten at least nine hours each night. But for some reason, that just wasn't possible this summer. I tried, really. It's not like I didn't want to sleep. Of course I did, but no matter how long I would lay in bed, I couldn't seem to manage more than five hours of sleep each night. Truthfully, I was annoyed. But what could I do? I had more important things on my mind than catching up on a few needless hours of sleep. I had to plan my food intake for the following day. Not to mention all the calculating I had to do for the foods I'd already eaten. Then, of course I'd have to think up an exercise routine and ways to get around family meals. I grew restless. I tossed and turned for hours in anticipation of the next day. My mind constantly wandered to my weight. When had my weight gone up? When had it gone down? What did I do to keep the number the same? Why was I one weight in the morning but then another weight at night? Obviously, I had a lot to figure out. So you see, sleep just wasn't that important anymore. My mom called it insomnia. Apparently I had insomnia. Whatever, I thought. Who cares if I have a sleeping problem? At least I'm losing weight. Life is better than ever. Nothing could faze me.

But there was one crucial fact that almost had me worried. As July rolled in with its patriotic boom and increasing summer heat, a bewildering observation haunted my thoughts. It all came about when I overheard my friend declaring her need for a tampon. It seemed like forever since I had needed one for myself. But I was probably just hallucinating. It had probably been four weeks ago. I'd get it in a few days, I was sure of it. But, just to make sure, I pulled out my dusty calendar and cautiously flipped through each month.

May. Early May to be exact. That was my last marked period. I must've forgotten to mark one because May didn't make sense. That was two months ago. Oh, but I knew, didn't doctors say your period could come irregularly the first year or so? Yeah, that had to be it. That's the only explanation. But wait, I thought carefully, that can't be the reason. I got my period three years ago. No way was it still irregular. Besides, it never had been before, so why would this month be different.

And then I remembered. As the thought crossed my mind a flash of fear struck me like a jolt of electricity. I recalled a piece of information from a health class that past year. It was amazing that I remembered. In fact, I astounded myself by having proof of learning; I never listened in that class. It was all about don't smoke, don't drink, don't do this, and don't do that. I already knew how to "say no to drugs" so was there even a use in paying attention? Yet shockingly, it appears I had. Thinking back on that class, I remembered hearing that the three causes of a lost period were pregnancy, over-exercising, and developing an eating disorder.

I crossed out that first reason right away. I knew I wasn't pregnant. The only way that was possible was if I had been drugged and raped. And I was pretty sure that wasn't the case. Actually, I was positive.

Reason number two was unlikely as well. I had only been running in soccer practice, soccer games, and about three times a week around the neighborhood. While this may be a tad more running than I had done in the past, it definitely wasn't enough of a difference to cause such a drastic situation.

The third cause made me frown with anguish. Eating disorder. The phrase hovered over me, briefly haunting my perspective on the past year. But that was only for a second. I quickly nixed the idea, kicking it under the rug, and erasing it from my thoughts.

You're just remembering it wrong. I assured myself. *That's not what the health teacher said at all. No, of course not. All she said was that loss of period could be a result of weight loss. Nothing wrong with that. You should be proud you lost weight. It means you're a good person.*

Suddenly my missed period didn't seem so bad. It was just a sign I had lost some weight. It was no big deal. It just meant I was eating healthier. In fact, it could even be considered a good sign. Just like the constant cold feeling and the lack of sleep. Yes, that was it; those symptoms were nothing to worry about. Somehow, in my twisted way of thinking, it all made sense. I didn't need reasoning and I didn't need proof. I told myself those signs were nothing but signs of success and nothing could convince me otherwise. Once again, I told myself lies, believing each one without a hint of doubt.

Road Trip

We were at a party when the brilliant idea occurred to us. Meredith and I lay in our sleeping bags in the corner of our room. She had been my good friend for over a year and recently we had grown even closer—we always turned to one another for support. As we each fought with our other friends, we confided in one another and I knew she always had my back. And on that particular night we were turning to each other once again.

We had felt excluded throughout the whole party, so when the other girls went off to take silly pictures, Mere and I went to talk about the one show we loved the most, *One Tree Hill.* How could you not love a show full of good-looking boys, intense family battles, and twisted love triangles? Top that off with one Chad Michael Murray and there you have it—the best show I've ever watched. Mere and I were hooked. So as we sat there discussing how cool it would be to meet the cast, I remembered something vital I had heard recently. The show was filmed in Wilmington, North Carolina. That was only a six- or seven-hour drive from our house. Summer was just around the corner; maybe we could go! But that would be a long shot. The trip would be long for either of our parents to travel. Even more, why would they agree to take two starry-eyed, obsessive girls to the set of a teen drama? But we had to try. Going there together would be the trip of a lifetime.

The next day I wriggled in between my mom and my dog and tentatively told her I had a proposition. I begged, I pleaded, and I even offered to do extra chores! All I wanted was to go for just one weekend. I'm almost certain that I broke the world record for the "most times within a five-minute span that someone says the word please."

I didn't get the answer I wanted right away. But with a lot of convincing and a lot of patience, I finally got my parents to agree. And when Meredith's parents gave her permission to go, I felt as though I was floating into the gorgeous sky. This would kick ass. We would stand on the infamous basketball court, take a studio tour, and get our pictures taken outside the "homes" of the characters. Maybe we would even meet the cast!

Okay, so maybe the cast idea didn't work out, but we got to accomplish all our other goals while we were there. But some unexpected events took place as well. When you're living the life of an oblivious anorexic, surprises should be suspected. My first mistake was looking up restaurants in Wilmington ahead of time. By doing that I planned where we would eat each day for lunch and each night for dinner. I even looked at menus online and planned what I would order weeks in advance. Needless to say, not everyone was on the same page. As the first lunch rolled around, we were nowhere near the place I had planned to eat. There were other restaurant, but none I wanted to go to. I begged to go somewhere else. Of course, this didn't turn out to well considering we were surrounded by places to eat and leaving seemed irrational. Or at least it did to everyone else. To me though, it seemed irrational to stay. I had already planned to eat elsewhere. That was the only way to go. But it was four against one. I trudged into a near by café and ordered with regret. The whole day I found myself feeling anxious and short-tempered, but I couldn't figure out why. However, I was certain that if I had eaten where I had planned, the day would have been much better.

Later that day we found ourselves in a mall. A sudden whiff of freshly baked cookies filled my nose as a breathed in. I turned around and saw my brother running toward the place responsible for this delicious yet terrifying smell. It was a cookie stand with every kind of cookie imaginable. My parents followed in my brother's footsteps, pulling out their wallets as they went. Meredith waited for me as I slowly sauntered along after them.

"All right everyone, pick out a cookie. It's on me." *This can't be happening,* I thought. *What do I do? Ah, you better think fast Nicole—it's your turn to order!"*

An animal-like groan escaped my mouth followed by a sudden "I have the worst stomachache." I grasped my stomach for effect and averted my eyes to the hard tile below me. They looked at me as if waiting for another answer, a real answer. But when nothing more came, they spoke with sadness in their voices. They told me to feel better and then handed over shiny coins to the cashier to round off their payment.

It was the first time that envy tempted me to disobey my eating disorder. I sat watching the gooey chocolate drip from their chins. The crumbs fell to the ground as they vigorously munched away. It wasn't fair. How could they spontaneously eat a cookie? If I ate a cookie, I would gain a pound right then and there. That's why I couldn't eat a cookie. If I ate one, I'd want more. And if I ate more, I'd get fat. So I sat there with jealousy creeping down from my head to my toes. The only reason I continued resisting temptation was the memory of how good I felt when I stepped on a scale and saw my weight drop. That would never happen again if I ate the cookie. It was just one stinking cookie. It was one cookie out of one day out of one year. Yet in that moment, it made all the difference. At that moment, that cookie was the deciding factor on whether I was a decent person or not.

Decent. I didn't even feel worthy of that in the next few days. My attempt at a nice run on the beach with Meredith was cut short by the ridiculously hot weather and the lure of the cool ocean waves. On top of that, I hadn't been getting in my daily number of sit-ups. My stomach would lose its muscle and I'd look fat. I was sure of it. However, I tried not to let this fear break me. My mom had a watchful eye on me and any waver might send her into disaster mode. I had to appear normal. For some reason, she had recently been pestering me with questions about a possible eating disorder. Well, I was positive that I didn't have that and somehow I had to make her positive too. Anxiety attacks over lack of exercise and surprise food offers would just not cut it on this vacation.

So far, the vacation had been amazing. Seeing the settings of our favorite TV show was even better than I imagined. But I couldn't shake the tense feeling that erupted at even the slightest mention of food. I struggled during each meal, trying to eat enough to please my mom. I was sure that I was succeeding though. I was eating way more than usual; I didn't think my mom would worry. Then why did she keep arguing with me? Even though I felt as if I was constantly cramming my mouth full, my mom continued to push me to eat more. Sheesh, nothing was ever good enough for her, was it?

As the vacation neared its end, we began our drive up north for Camp Silver Beach. One of my best friends was there at a sleep-away camp and I would soon join her. About a mile from the camp and an hour before check-in, we decided to stop for lunch. We found a cozy seafood restaurant and plopped into our seats impatiently awaiting the waiter. When he brought the biscuits out, I decided there was no way I would have one. I sat and listened to the others talk, trying to distract myself from the food I knew was on its way. When the salad was set down in front of me, I gasped. It was huge. This dinner must've been designed for giants. No way was I eating even a fourth of that massive meal. So, as usual, I began to slowly nibble at the food in front of me, stopping every so often to sip my Diet Coke and talk. As I declared myself finished, I caught my mother shake her head in disapproval. I tried to throw that out of my mind. I was about to go to camp. I would be free from her supervision and I would have the power to make up for all the food I had eaten that weekend to try and please her. I would have a lot of work to do that coming week to make up for slacking off.

Sleep-away

We pulled into the camp and I stepped out into the scorching summer air. I took a deep breath, noting the intense smell of pine trees as I did so. I admired the rows of cabins surrounding me while also taking note of the soccer field to my left. I stood still for a moment, listening to the distant squeals of laughter.

The laughter reminded me of elementary school. Random, I know. But the shrieking shouts of happiness took me back to recess. I was running around playing tag without a care in the world. The person who was "it" made a beeline for me. I wheeled around and bolted away, tripping on a stick as I went. I fell, tumbling down on top of another girl. Our classmates wait, unsure of what to do. But then, out of nowhere, there's a faint giggle. The giggle begins to build into a laugh. Suddenly she is surrounded by dozens of unique laughs, creating a symphony of joy.

A smiling counselor swoops in front of me ripping me out of my dream and back to reality. Those days are long gone. They were replaced with days full of pressure, drama, and hard work. But this week was about forgetting that. This was camp. This week I would be free from my parents and free from school. Sadly though, I would not be free from my eating disorder. Unknowingly, it had managed its way into my suitcase and it was there to stay.

A girl screamed my name. I knew that voice and I returned it with my own squeal of delight. She was the reason I came. Going to camp together was her idea. It sounded ideal at the time. We hugged as though we hadn't seen each other for years. We ran into the cabin and I heard the same laughter I had so longingly hoped for. Only this time I was producing it, not witnessing it. The happiness began to emerge. This was going to be a great week; I could tell already.

At dinner I ate french fries. It was one of my "bad" foods, so of course, I couldn't eat anything else if I wanted to enjoy them. It would be my one splurge of the week. It would be my one rebellious rule break. I felt as though I was eating like a whale. Maybe that's why everyone was staring. Maybe they think I'm eating like a whale too. I didn't want to give off a bad first impression. I thought I better stop. And although my stomach growled for more food, I threw the fries away and felt pride settle in. But even after disposing of the sinful food, I still noticed disapproving glances shooting from my campmates eyes. *Weird,* I thought. *Wonder what's eating them. Then again, who cares?*

But the disapproving glares were just beginning. The next morning I received double the amount when I nibbled on an apple for breakfast. I noted observantly what others around me were eating. My friend was to my left, having her second bowl of cereal, with a waffle waiting for her on the plate. Across from me, there were girls with doughnuts and milk cartons. There were even girls with cereal, waffles, doughnuts, and milk cartons. I looked down at my apple one more time. I couldn't help thinking how much stronger I was than all of them. It was weird to realize, but I found myself building up a wall of confidence. I never felt confident. This was a feeling I had been missing out on. If I wanted to keep it, I knew I had to keep up with my food restrictions.

Now sure, the camp had many adventurous activities to offer. And I was more than ready to take them on. In one week I managed to go "sharking" several times, a process where you ride on a long tube that's attached to a speeding motorboat. I learned how to skateboard, I played multiple games of street hockey, and I went sailing for my first time. Yet in spite of all my new adventures, there was an obvious tension building between my good friend and I.

She was obsessed with her camera. Everywhere we went she had to take ten more pictures. Afterward, each one would be thoroughly evaluated. If she didn't like it, that picture was out. But, if I didn't like it, too bad. It was probably a good thing that she had her rule. If she deleted all the pictures I thought I looked bad in, well at the end of the day, she'd end up with none. So that was how it was. We took pictures. I looked bad. She didn't care. The picture was saved. As we took these pictures, a reoccurring comment shot out of my friend's mouth like rapid fire.

"Ewwwwwww. Look at your arm in that picture! That's the most disgusting thing I've ever seen! You're disgustingly skinny!"

She would go on and on like this, making me more uncomfortable by the second. Occasionally she'd throw in a "you should eat more" but those tips were lost behind her constant insults. With each statement about my "gross skinniness," my self-esteem shot lower and lower to the ground. She was right. I was ugly. I did look gross. But, at least she thinks I'm skinny. That's the only compliment she had given me. That must mean that's my only good quality. I can't let that success be overshadowed by my failures. I guess the only option was to be skinnier.

I pushed myself hard that week, eating less than I ever had before. Each comment pushed me harder. Each day I would watch those around me indulge themselves in junk as I nibbled on my fruits and veggies. Yet as hard as I tried, I couldn't ignore what she said. Her insults rang out through my head, stinging me hard.

For my eating disorder, restricting food was not enough. Increasing exercise was essential. Unfortunately, going for runs wasn't exactly easy at this camp. There were kids everywhere. There was no possible route that wouldn't intersect with dozens of screaming campers. I had to jump at every little opportunity I could get. When a ball was accidentally tossed, hit, or kicked twenty yards from the field or court I jumped at the chance to go fetch it. People showered me with thanks for retrieving the ball but little did they know it was completely my pleasure. In fact, I had to hold myself back from thanking them in return.

My best opportunity came at night. There was a camp-wide scavenger hunt in which each cabin was a team. As each group disbanded and began their quest for victory, my counselor decided we needed to build up some team spirit. A silly song was quickly invented and everyone began to belt out the tune. At first we marched along chanting our song with an unusual combination of both pride and embarrassment. Then the leader suggested we run to the next clue. My ears perked up at the word and I cheered up for the first time that night.

"Great idea! It will help us get there faster. Plus, come on, the exercise won't hurt us." I attempted to silence the groans that filled the crisp night sky. Lucky for me, the counselor was on my side. We began to trot along at a slow pace. I was ahead of the pack. As the wind blew my hair back and cooled off my sweaty face, I felt a sense of peace rush through me. The grasshoppers' chirps began playing their own song. The fireflies were like tiny explosions, popping up at every corner. The stars shone down on me and I drifted away. Suddenly I was picking up speed. My feet were uncontrollable and I heard myself laugh as I sped into the night. I didn't have to look at myself to know that the hugest smile was plastered on my face. And then a yell interrupted me.

"Nicole! Nicole, slow down! You're losing us." Damn. I had forgotten where I was for a moment. But as much as I wanted to be elsewhere, I was still here, still at camp. And when I looked back, I realized how fast I had gone. They were way back at the beginning of the trail. I halted with disappointment. Guess this wasn't going to be the much-needed run I was hoping for. When the others finally caught up to me I was even more discouraged to hear that, due to a girl falling and scraping her knee, there would be no more running for the night. What could I do? I had to continue on. But that excitement, that freedom that appeared during my lightning run, never returned to me. The rest of the night was a letdown. Just like the camp.

New York City

I jumped off my bed and slid over to my dresser. I wrapped my hand around the white knob and opened the top drawer, scrambling through my old, ratty T-shirts.

Where is it, I asked myself as I frantically continued the search, *Come on, come on, come on. I know it's in here somewhere.*

My hand fell on yet another white shirt. I looked more closely and saw a red heart peeking out from the pile. I touched the shirt with hope. Yanking it out, I smiled to myself as I admired my discovery. The shirt read: "I love NYC." My dad had gotten it for me on a business trip a of couple years back. I had always felt like a phony when wearing it since I'd never even been to New York before. But this time, I put it on with confidence. Tomorrow was the day. Tomorrow I would finally get to see the city I had heard so much about. We were going for just a weekend, accompanied by my dad's parents. His mom, my Grams, had always been a New Yorker at heart. She loved the city and loved telling me tales of her many adventures there. Ever since I can remember, she had wanted to take me. When my parents announced the trip, excitement began to build inside of me.

We were taking a train. It would leave around ten in the morning, so we would eat breakfast at the train station before we left. At least, that was my parents' plan. But you know me, always having to have my own way when it came to food. I slyly insisted I would eat breakfast at home. Thinking back, I don't remember the excuse I used, although at that point, it probably didn't matter. My parents were already certain of what was happening to me, even if I wasn't. But silly me, I still thought that I could fool them. I woke up early and made my way into the kitchen while my parents were preoccupied with last-minute packing. I took out a bowl and poured some milk into it. Then I took out a spoon and plopped it in the milk lake I had created. I carefully set the bowl in the sink and hurried away. Later on, when my parents asked what I had done for breakfast, I crisply replied, "I had cereal. Check the sink."

The vacation began with that simple little lie but it would end with pure deception. Each meal required another story. Each food required another excuse. On that first night we spent almost an hour walking up and down Times Square, looking for a place to eat. Everywhere we went was either too crowded or too fancy. I kept urging that we should give up and "settle for a pretzel from the street vendor." The search for food was becoming tedious, and we had a Broadway show to catch in a few hours. Time was running out and we had to make a decision. A pizza joint appeared in front of us. The emptiness should've served as a warning, but instead it served as a reason to go. We piled into a booth and swatted away the flies surrounding our table. As we looked at the menus, I found myself panicking with pressure. I had no clue what to order and couldn't help feeling rushed. But clearly, I had time. There wasn't a waiter in sight and it looked as if the quick dinner we hoped for just wouldn't happen.

Yet still, I faced the dilemma of choice. No way was I eating pizza. Greasy, fatty, cheesy—pizza was a triple threat. I turned the menu over to the pasta side and put my finger on the first meat-free option I saw. It was linguini pasta with cream sauce and veggies. Normally, I would immediately cross this option off the list because of the cream sauce; however, this trip I had to be different. I knew from my daily weigh-ins that last week at camp resulted in a pretty solid weight loss. To me this was great, but the accomplishment would need to be reversed. I had another doctor's appointment the day after we got home from New York. My appointments were becoming more frequent, and I knew I had to gain some weight if I ever wanted to get them off my back. So I went for it. I broke the rules and ordered the dish. To me, ordering it was a feat in itself. The amount I ate wouldn't matter, even if I ate one or two bites of the calorie-packed pasta I was sure I'd gain a little weight. And as soon as I was served, I knew that was exactly what I would do. I would eat several bites just to satisfy my parents, but that was it. Eating at all was bad enough. So I resorted to my usual twirling and picking until everyone else around me was finished. I felt horrible. I felt fat. I had eaten creamy pasta sauce. At least it would shut my mom up. If I felt that horrible then she must have felt content. Or so I thought, until her words brought me back to reality.

"No way are you finished with that." As she spoke, I noticed her fighting back tears. "You better start eating right now or we'll just go back to the hotel. I don't even think you ate five bites of that." This was so confusing. How could she say that? I had eaten half the plate! What was she talking about? I gasped at her anger as I desperately looked around for support. But it seemed as though everyone was on her side. They pushed me to eat until I flat-out refused to go on. I felt broken. A scream built up inside me but I swallowed it back down. I fought back the tears and let out an angry grunt. Silence took over and I sat there frowning until the check was paid and we left.

That night we watched the Broadway musical *Xanadu*. It was funny, entertaining, and everything we had hoped for. Yet, despite the laughter, I still felt a sense of sadness. I looked in front of me. Two children were fighting over their box of Skittles. They each had a soda in their laps and a grin on their young faces. I was envious. I wanted more than anything to enjoy food again. No, I would not admit I was anorexic. That wasn't the problem. There had to be another explanation. But I couldn't deny that my relationship with food had changed. I didn't enjoy it anymore. All food gave me were pounds of guilt and loads of stomachaches. Food had become my enemy.

The next morning we woke up early with a full agenda. We scrambled for our places on the crowded subway and rode with excitement. Our destination was Ellis Island. As we stood there, dumbfounded, staring with awe into the crowd, we realized the quest for a ticket would not be easy. In fact, just waiting in line for a ticket would take all day. We quickly moved to plan B. We would take a ferry around Ellis Island and under the Brooklyn Bridge. That way, we could still get good pictures and see the sights while managing to save a huge amount of time. Plan B turned out perfectly. The ferry ride was magnificent and ended just in time for lunch. As we slowly drifted back to the dock, I found my thoughts drifting along with the boat. Reminders of my upcoming doctor's appointment flooded my head. I determined that I could not show up on Monday with another weight loss appearing on the scale. I had to eat. I could break the rules just this once and what better place to do so than in New York.

I quickly learned how wrong I was. New York had plenty of choices—that was the problem. The types of food and where to eat overwhelmed me. Without realizing it, I began calculating which restaurant was the healthiest and how much I would allow myself to eat. My plan to break the rules was forced from my mind and replaced by the demands of my disorder.

The rest of the week only got worse. It was obvious my family was becoming fed up with my constant pestering about food.

"Where are we eating? When are we eating? Where are we eating later today? Are we getting a dessert tonight? What's happening for breakfast tomorrow?" I couldn't stop myself. It was as if I was under a spell. The questions kept flying out of my mouth only to be returned with raised eyebrows and annoyed faces. But for some reason, I didn't understand why the faces staring back at me were so tense. To me, these questions were necessary. Asking them went without saying. They just needed to be answered. That was all. I wasn't crazy for wondering, I was just being smart.

It was no surprise to anyone when we returned the following Monday only to find that I had lost more weight. The doctor was fed up. My mom was fed up. Even my dad was beginning to show more worry. To them, another weight loss was not an option. I couldn't understand what the big deal was. I was just becoming healthier, why didn't they see that? Why couldn't they realize I was perfectly normal? Everyone my age ate like that. I was sure of it. But then again, a part of me questioned if that was really true. If it was, then why wasn't everyone losing weight like me?

You're just being silly. Of course they lose weight too. You just don't know about it because their parents aren't being so overprotective and dramatic about it like your parents are. And just like that my eating disorder shot down my doubts once again. Just like that, I went back to believing that life was great and nothing was wrong. Just like that, I blinded myself from the truth.

Tryouts

All summer, I had been training for soccer tryouts. My high school was known for having a solid girl's soccer team and I knew it would be hard to even make JV. But that was my goal, and nothing was going to get between me and my goal. I began running three times a week. Each one was a struggle because I would run out in the heat of the July or August air with nothing in me to use as fuel. If I did decide to eat a little snack beforehand I'd always make sure to counteract it with a longer run. Each time I grew tired or weary, I reminded myself of my ultimate goal—making the team and starting high school off with a bang. I set up private lessons with a trainer, went to the conditioning workouts, and practiced tricks out in my front yard. Making the team was serious to me.

As tryouts drew closer, my mom's doubts about letting me participate reached a whole new level. Before, the issue of her letting me try out was just one of her petty worries, nothing to be afraid of. But recently it had become a threat. As we sat in the doctor's office, yet again, my chance at trying out was put on the line. I grimaced as I listened to my mom talk to the doctor. She expressed her fear that I wasn't healthy enough to do the required two-a-days. And she was afraid that I would lose an immense amount of weight if I did play. I waited with anticipation for the doctor's all mighty response.

"She should be fine. She's agreed to eat more for the tryouts, and since nothing has been determined yet there's no reason not to let her." As the lady spoke I fought the urge to run up and hug her. I smugly turned toward my mom to give her the signature "told you so" face. Like I said before, nothing (and no one) would get between me and my goal.

The following morning, I forced myself to scarf down a piece of toast before running out the door and arriving at the field. Once there, my anxiety began to kick in. There were tons of girls all over. This would not be an easy competition. Everyone was smiling and talking, but the mood was determined and intense. Each girl wanted to stand out. Each girl was fighting for the same prize. I prepared myself as the coach walked over to the bleachers and began splitting us into grades.

Our first task was to run one and a half miles in twelve minutes. This feat was one I had practiced in advance. Multiple times in the past week I had gotten my dad to drive me up to the track and time me as I attempted it. I only failed one time; coincidentally, that was the one time I didn't eat anything prior to the run. I wasn't worried. I ate that piece of toast for a reason and here was my chance to burn it off. I pushed myself hard as I sped past those around me. I kept a steady pace, realizing that if I constantly went fast I'd soon be worn out. As the whistle blew to signal the end of the twelve minutes, I beamed with pride looking back at the finish line I had already passed. Tryouts were off to a good start, but there was a long way to go and I was already hungry for more fuel.

After the morning practice, I mustered up courage to ask my mom for a bowl of buttered pasta. Both butter and pasta were against the rules, but at that moment I couldn't have cared less. To me, making that soccer team was way more important than listening to my rules about what to restrict and how much. From experience I had learned that I needed the energy from food if I wanted to keep up my strength for the try-outs. So I ate the pasta with only a small amount of guilt. The guilt was small only because I knew that I'd quickly burn off those calories. I knew what was in store and I was ready for it.

The next few days were tough. All around me girls were growing tired. The heat tore us apart and the humidity drenched us with sweat. We went home hopeful as we awaited the dreaded first cuts to be posted. When I read my name on the computer screen my heart leaped out of my chest. I began jumping up and down and squealing with excitement. But it was just the beginning. I had two more painful days to go before final cuts and I wasn't sure if I could make it. I ate at each meal in hopes that my sacrifice would be rewarded. I ran as hard as I could and played with intensity. Only four more girls would be cut and I could not let myself be one of them. I needed this. I needed to be told that I was good enough. I needed proof that I wasn't as worthless as I always felt. I needed to know that I wasn't a complete failure.

But I was. I was a complete failure. The list was posted and I wasn't on it. I read the results over and over hoping that my name would appear on that list. I hated myself. I know I said that multiple times before, but that time I actually meant it. I thought I hated myself before, but that was nothing. Now I really hated myself. Now I was worth nothing.

The disappointment struck me hard. The only way I knew how to cope was to eat less and less. I was aware that later in the week I would meet with a specialist at Children's National Medical Center who my doctor had recommended. But frankly, that just didn't matter. I was scum. I was nothing. I needed to restrict. I needed to diet. I needed more than anything to see myself lose more weight. Maybe I couldn't have the final say in who made the team, but at least I could always have the final say in what I ate. Maybe I sucked at soccer, but at least I didn't suck at resisting the temptations of food. I needed to prove that to myself. I needed to know there was something inside me worth living for.

But soon I learned that I was looking in all the wrong places. I had no control. I was merely a puppet. Weight loss wouldn't bring me that desired happiness. Restricting wouldn't prove that I was strong. No, that was not the way. Everything was a lie. I soon learned that I had to use all of my strength to fight back, and all the control I ever wanted was just around the corner. I would discover this truth over the next year. It would emerge from the difficult depths of recovery. It would emerge from the endurance of pain. It would emerge from the inevitable suffering.

Treatment

Diagnosis

Today was the day. It was the day we had all been waiting for. It was the day that matters would be thrown into someone else's hands. It was the day we met with a specialist. My pediatrician had finally given up and recommended us to Dr. Silber, a doctor at Children's National Medical Center in Washington, DC. I was certain he would prove my parents wrong. I had it all planned out. I would meet him, get some blood tests taken, maybe get a stomach exam, and then he would find it—the reason for my weight loss. Whether it was a type of cancer or a problem with my thyroid gland, I didn't care. In fact, I found myself hoping he would find some sort of flesh-eating disease. At least then my parents would finally see that I was telling the truth. I absolutely did not have an eating disorder. If I did then I would know about it. And I didn't, so there had to be some other cause.

We met him two days before the start of my freshman year. Orientation had just ended and we made a pit stop for lunch along the way. The impending "weigh-in" caused me to go out on a limb. For the first time in a while, I went to a restaurant and ordered something other than salad. The location was Panera Bread and the culprit was black bean soup. The "L" followed by the "F" on the menu signified that the soup was low in fat. Only for that reason, I allowed myself to take a chance and order it. As I scolded myself for being so daring, I noticed my parents exchanged a disapproving glance. It seemed as though nothing I did was good enough for them. Nothing I did could make them happy.

I stared at the soup and slurped it slowly as my parents tore apart their sandwiches. The bread they had given me to accompany the soup was pushed aside to the far left corner. I placed it there not a second after receiving my tray. My only focus was the soup. That was hard enough. So I ate until I felt like I was going to explode. My stomach was bloated and my legs began to look like balloons. I was fat. Before I was worthy, now I was nothing.

I darted my eyes toward the enemy. The soup glared back as steam rose up from its center. It was only half empty yet I felt completely full. How could that be? I decided that the amount they gave was not normal. It was possible my parents had even secretly told the workers to give me extra. It wouldn't surprise me considering how desperate they had been for me to eat over the past few months. But it was okay. Everything was okay. Today I would prove them wrong. By nightfall they would apologize while promising never to doubt me again.

One long car ride, two hours of waiting, and three nurses later, he was there. The man was standing in front of us, but he wasn't real. He couldn't be. The man I expected was grouchy and mean. He wore a scowl on his face and showed disgust at my weight and at my situation. The man in front of me wasn't like that at all. He was smiling brightly and showering us with welcomes. In a funny accent that I would soon come to love, he apologized for being late. He seemed genuinely concerned and determined to find us an answer. After looking over my vital signs and talking privately to both me and to my parents, he suddenly declared that he had one. Just like that, no tests and no x-rays. Nothing was going according to plan.

The next hour was full of confusion, despair, disappointment, and anger. The first thing I remember him talking about was "malnutrition." Apparently I had that, whatever that was. But I didn't have to wonder long, I shortly found out in gruesome detail. My body didn't have enough nutrition in it so it had prepared itself for death. Over time, with lack of food, my stomach, my heart, and my liver all began to shrink. For that reason, my heart rate was indisputably low and the amount of food I could endure was becoming lower along with it. I was lacking in fats and had become severely underweight. He took out some growth charts, which plotted my weight in comparison to other girls my age. At the beginning, my weight had been just over the fiftieth percentile. Now, however, it was half as much.

Luckily, he explained that I wasn't yet to a point where hospitalization was needed. I could stay at home and go to school but crucial changes would have to be made.

Change number one: no physical activity until further notice.

Yes, that included soccer, running, and even participating in gym class at school. As he outlined this particular rule, I felt as though my world was crumbling. I was spinning into a black hole. Nothing mattered. Nothing mattered without soccer. I'd be out for at least a season, he told us with regret. It was necessary for my health. I knew he was right, but all I felt was anger. How could this happen? What did I do to deserve this? Without warning, the tears began to flood down my face. The sympathetic people surrounding me offered tissues. My parents were obviously fighting back tears of their own. But they didn't understand, no one could understand. Soccer meant everything to me, and now I had nothing. And not to mention gym! How embarrassing! Everyone would pester me with questions about why I never joined in. The teacher wouldn't care because Dr. Silber guaranteed us he'd write the school a note. But what would I tell the kids? How could I explain sitting on the sidelines? Did I even want to? And how the hell was I supposed to survive without soccer?

Suddenly, the room began to spin. Confusion engulfed me. I felt as if a vortex was opening up ready to swallow me whole. Questions soared through my mind; yet, the only word I seemed to speak was "NO." The main sounds that filled the room were my desperate sobs and the uncomfortable shuffling of the doctor across the table. I was positive that this was the ultimate bad news. But I soon found it was only going to get worse.

Change number two: all meals were decided and supervised by the parents.

Now while this did sound terrible, at first I found change one more unmanageable. Dr. Silber assured me that he had clearly laid out the guidelines of an appropriate meal plan when he met with my parents alone. He also clarified that due to my shrunken stomach I would have to gradually work up to the new eating habits. Luckily, the doctor told my parents to start feeding me small meals, slowly increasing my intake each day. That didn't sound too bad. I mean how much food could it be? I felt relief spread through my body only to be interrupted by the doctor's serious tone.

"This will be the hardest thing Nicole has ever done. It will be the hardest thing this family has ever done. There will be times when she might even want to die. There will be times when progress may not seem possible. There is a chance you may find it easier to admit her into a hospital. If that is the case we will make that happen right away. Just remember, be patient. Always have patience with Nicole. This is not her fault, and she is not responsible for her actions. I will say this one more time: it will be the hardest thing any of you have ever done."

His words were severe but none of us could have guessed how right he was. We left the office in shock, too stunned to speak. At least it had been verified that an eating disorder was not the problem. He said it himself—I had "malnutrition," not anorexia. I was sick, not possessed. Finally my parents were proven wrong. I continued to think this as I trudged into our house and stomped up the stairs. As I went, something peculiar caught my eye. At that moment, I let it be, knowing that my parents were just around the corner. I promised myself I would go back and check it out as soon as I had some space.

That night I crept downstairs and shuffled my way into the darkness of the living room. I slapped my hand along the wall as I desperately searched for the light switch. As the lamps turned on and color returned from hiding, I directed my focus to the coffee table. Tearing through the stack of papers that lay on top, I finally found what I was looking for. It was a paper with the bold heading: "How to feed your anorexic." Suddenly, I remembered.

I was back in that office drying my tears as we prepared to leave. Out of the corner of my eye I saw a hand reach out. It was the doctor. He was handing my mom a pamphlet. I turned toward the door and my mother appeared behind me. She took me in her arms as we walked tiredly out of the room.

I returned to my living room with shock. Was this the paper he had handed her? Was this the truth of today's visit? Was it possible that I was anorexic?

No. It couldn't be. There was no way. My mom must have picked up this paper on her own when she was so sure I had that problem. This paper was worthless now. It didn't mean anything. The doctor said I was malnourished. That's all. I was just malnourished.

First Weeks

The first meal in the long journey of recovery was pizza. I admit it I entered that first meal with no clue of what was happening. I was still in denial. I was still oblivious to my eating disorder. But clearly, I was not the only clueless one. The fact that my parents chose pizza for that first meal exhibits their sheer inexperience at dealing with an anorexic. The only thing worse than pizza would be topping it off with a glass of soda and a piece of chocolate cake.

The idea was to start off small. So when my parents placed the pizza in front of me, I was sure it was all just one cruel joke. Pizza of all things! That was my ultimate "bad food." It was my ultimate fear. I had no doubt in my mind that eating that pizza would cause me to gain back all the weight I had lost, that's how powerful pizza was to me. Doughy, greasy, cheesy—each word was its own mini-nightmare, but together it was a deadly sin. The smell of the fresh pie tickled my nose, triggering a typhoon of tears. It was my first time crying at the sight of my meal. It was the first, but most definitely not the last. My parents seemed uptight.

My parents tried hard to follow the doctor's orders to be patient with me. Yet, despite their best efforts, I could sense the annoyance in their eyes. I knew what they were thinking. *Why is she in hysterics over a piece of pizza? She must be going insane!* I knew these were their thoughts because they were my thoughts too. I had no idea what I was doing. I had no idea why the pizza scared me as much as it did.

But there was no denying it, that pizza and me were not going to get along. I had to get myself away from it and fast. Desperately, I ran through strategies in my mind. I spoke carefully as I remembered facts from the earlier doctor's appointment.

"Remember my stomach is extra-small. I can't handle all this food yet. I think I might throw up. Please let me be finished!" I sobbed as I begged them to let me off the hook. I watched as their faces softened, my first sign of success. Their eyes were sympathetic as my mom wiped away my tears. I was free. I won. I am better than the pizza. I am better than my parents. No one tells me what to do.

The days went on and nothing changed. I had found my way to keep control and nothing could stop me now. Each meal, each food, became another sob story. My stomach always ached and the tears were always there. My parents always agreed and I was always saved from the horrors of eating.

I did eat however. To me it seemed as if that was all I ever did. Just the fact that I was eating breakfast was enough to make me want to die. School had started but it felt as though my life had been put on pause. Every day was a battle to focus. All I could think about was what I had eaten, what they would make me eat next, and what line I could use to get out of it. The schoolwork didn't matter. The teacher didn't matter. The lessons didn't matter. Even my friends didn't seem to matter. All that mattered was food. All that mattered was losing more weight. My eating disorder took full control of my life, but I still trudged along in denial.

One day I came home to the smell of soup. Immediate panic settled in as I prayed that my nose was only playing tricks on me. Every day I had a peanut butter sandwich. Every day my mom cut off the crust. Every day I convinced her I could only eat half. That was how it was and even that felt like too much. But as I suspected, that day was different. That day my mom made soup. It was unexpected and new. I couldn't handle it. Before I knew what I was doing, I threw myself onto the floor and began to scream. I had no idea what was happening. I was lying there, kicking and screaming like a grouchy four-year-old. I knew I was being stupid, but for some reason, I just couldn't stop. I was desperate. I was terrified. I could not, I repeated could NOT, eat that soup. I demanded my sandwich. I demanded normal. I could not combine change and food. Change was hard. Food was harder. But change with food was downright impossible for me. After thirty minutes of torture, my mom finally caved in. She whipped up a sandwich and sat me down to eat. She was on her last straw and I knew any more fussing would send her overboard. I somehow managed to chew the sandwich in silence. Embarrassment at the scene I had just displayed took over. I was full of regret. I promised myself I would start to behave.

Then, just one day later, the Fritos came out. I counted nine. There were nine Fritos sprawled out on my plate and I was expected to eat every one. Again, I felt my body being abducted as I began to scream. My fists pounded the table. I shouted "NO" at the top of my lungs. I refused. I pleaded. I cried. And I cried some more. I could not eat those chips.

"This is my first time eating chips!" I screamed my proposal at the top of my lungs: "I can't eat nine on my first time. Remember what Dr. Silber said, I have to work my way up. Besides, my stomach is already full. Don't forget it's shrunken, okay?"

Miraculously, I ate five chips that day—five with the promise that there would be more to come. The next day six chips were on the plate. Again, I convinced my parents it was too much. Again, I ate five. Five became my number for the week. It wasn't until the following week that I finally agreed to eat six. But, of course, this accomplishment did not come without another outburst. My uncontrollable outbursts were starting to become a way of life.

This is all I remember from my first two weeks of high school. I couldn't tell you what new friends I made. I couldn't tell you what homework I had or which teachers learned each student's name. I couldn't tell you what I did during lunch or who I sat with. All I could tell you was that those weeks were hell. Those weeks were about food. Those weeks were about fighting. Those weeks were about crying.

Those weeks were just the beginning.

Ultimatum

The car ride was conquered by silence. Neither my mom nor I uttered a word. I had been taken out of school early and we were on our way to the follow-up appointment at a branch of the Children's National Medical Center in Spring Valley. We were about to meet with Dr. Silber for our second time. It was the moment of truth on our path to success. We turned away from the traffic of the highway and onto the desolate side roads of suburban Washington, DC. Arriving fifteen minutes early, we stepped out of the car and took a seat on the curb. As I suspected, my mom pulled out a paper bag. It was time for me to have my lunch. I forced it down with discomfort and battled my mom about the amount of my drink. The minutes passed slowly, but finally it was time to go in.

We climbed the stairs to the third level. With doubt about where to go, we searched the area surrounding us. We found our way and stepped into the waiting room filled with children's books and toys. After what seemed like an hour, I heard the funny but lovable voice of Dr. Silber as he rounded the corner. He ushered me into the room, right after taking my vitals. His face looked sad as he pored over his sheet. He spoke slowly as if choosing his words carefully.

"This is not going as I had hoped. I'm afraid you've lost three more pounds. If you keep losing at this rate, you'll be dead in a few more weeks. At this point I really feel that hospitalization is our best option."

A single tear ran down my cheek, and I shuddered as the warm drop landed on my thumb. At that point, describing my mom is near impossible. The only word that comes to mind is shocked. She was utterly and completely shocked. She sat motionless as she attempted to take it all in.

"I...I...uh...I...can't." My words were barely audible because my voice shook with fear. "Is...there anything else I can do? Please...anything...please."

He nodded with compassion as he presented me an ultimatum. There was only one other option. What I had been eating was not enough. What I had just eaten was not enough. I either had to go to the hospital or walk across the street to the deli and eat a second lunch. When I reminded him that I just ate, he didn't seem to care. A second lunch was necessary if I wanted to stay hospital-free. The choice was a lose-lose situation. I was torn inside, too scared to eat more and too scared to take it to the next level. I had to give the deli a try.

As we walked across to the deli my hand began to shake. I moaned and clenched my jaw, attempting to hold back my overwhelming emotions. My mom grabbed me and squeezed me tight. She still loved me. Everything was falling apart but at least someone still loved me. I tried to remember that as the garden burger was placed in front of me. A bag of chips lay next to it. I looked at it and became paralyzed. My mom urged me to start eating. We had to hurry; they were waiting for us over at the clinic. I yelled at her to give me time. I yelled at her to help me. I couldn't make this decision. I couldn't do it; she needed to do it for me. I yearned for her to give me her opinion. What did she want? What should I do? Would I be a failure if I ate this? Would I be a failure if I didn't? I needed to know. But she wouldn't tell me. This was something I had to decide for myself.

I was sure nothing could be worse than making this decision. I stared at the meal as memories of the lunch I had already eaten filled my brain. There was no way this was possible. The hospital seemed to be the easier option. I tried so hard to fight it. I tried so hard to think of another way. But there was nothing. I had nothing. This was what I needed to say.

"Let's go back. Let's tell them I'll go to the hospital. I'm just not strong enough for this." As I spoke, my mom whipped out her cell phone.

"Call your father. Let him know what's going on." She shoved the phone toward me only to get it shoved right back. I couldn't hear his voice. I couldn't even repeat my choice. She'd have to tell him. She'd have to let him know what a screw-up their daughter had become.

As we walked back up the stairs to the clinic, she assured me that my father would meet up with us as soon as possible. Her voice sounded so distant. I wondered if the love I'd recently felt was still there.

We told him. We told him and the deal was final. As Dr. Silber listed off the next steps to take, I was finally broken. I couldn't hold it back any longer. A sob burst out of me as I fell to the ground. I heard myself screaming for forgiveness, and I looked up with despair. For the first time, I noticed that another lady had walked into the room. She was a witness as I crumbled apart. That other lady was my future dietician. But, at that point, I couldn't care less about who she was or why she was there. All that mattered was what would happen to me. How long would I stay there? What would it be like? Was I going to die? The questions were infinite but I could barely comprehend the answers. My mind was spinning. Darkness enclosed me in a confined box of pain. Light disappeared and all hope was ripped away. Life had no more meaning. Death's appeal quickly grew. Fear weighed me down and disappointment swallowed me whole.

The dietician began to speak. "I'm very sorry about the situation, but I can assure you that you'll be taken good care of. While you stay at the hospital I'll be working with one of my colleagues to create your meal plan. It's not possible for you to have any say in your meals; however, you do get to pick three food items that we will never give you."

"But I'm a vegetarian!!!!!" The thought of eating poor, little animals filled me with disgust. I didn't think it was possible to feel anymore hate than I already did, but that information proved me wrong. No way would I let them serve me meat. No way.

But there was no use arguing, Dr. Silber moved on to his next explanation.

"You'll stay there just two or three days if all goes well. Each night a fluid will be pumped into you through a tube. The fluid will run for the whole night, and during the day you will eat three relatively small meals. The hope is to get you started on your weight gain and put you back on stable ground. Once that happens we will send you home. Possibly, the fluid and tube will have to come home with you. Don't be scared. Everything is going to be okay."

Nothing was going to be okay. Everything was one big nightmare. I pinched myself to make sure I wasn't dreaming. How did things get this bad? How did I let myself go this far? What was I thinking? What will I do?

At that moment, it finally clicked. As I crouched down on the floor, hysterically sobbing and gasping for breath, it finally clicked. As I looked up at my mom, watching her tear-up and stammer at me with fear, it finally clicked. As I was told my heart rate was incredibly low and if we didn't act soon I might die, it finally clicked. As we headed to the hospital with nothing but desperation, it finally clicked. I was anorexic. I am anorexic.

Hospital Entry

A series of piercing, periodic beeps awoke me from my restless sleep. My eyes fluttered open, half-awake, I momentarily forgot where I was. Full of confusion, I looked around at my surroundings. I felt something itching my nose and reached up to touch it. That's when I felt the tube. That's when I remembered. I tried to go back to sleep but the mat below me was lumpy and uncomfortable. I felt disgusting and was in desperate need of a shower. My dad was snoring on the pull-out mattress beside me, and I heard the jerky movements of the patient on the other side of the room. Sleep was not an option. Instead, I thought back on the past ten hours.

We had arrived at Children's National Medical Center around six o' clock. I entered the main lobby with tears stinging my eyes as I searched for my dad among the sea of people. When I saw his face, my eyes stung even more. He was stricken with worry and had the same blank stare I had noticed on my mom not too long ago. It wasn't until eight o' clock when we got into the first room. They told us we would have a private room, a coveted option that not many patients received.

The first few hours at the hospital were filled with nurses and doctors. One person came to take records, another to take my vitals, another to welcome me, and another to teach me about the nose tube. Not to mention the hospital director, an adolescent specialist, and a nutritionist also came by. By ten o'clock, I was sick and tired of describing why I was there and how I felt. I was tired of being told what would happen and how long it would take. I was tired of doctors and nurses, and I just wanted to go to sleep.

But it was clear the staff had other plans. They sent two young nurses to help me get the nose tube placed. It was inserted through my nostrils and ended in my stomach. Every night the nose tube was attached to a machine that pumped fluid into me via the tube. The fluid was a high-calorie supplement that was intended to help me gain weight. The idea seemed terrifying but yet somehow, it was also a relief. To know that I would have help gaining weight took a huge load off of my shoulders. I had failed at gaining weight on my own and I knew that I needed this kind of jump-start. But still, just thinking about the massive amounts of calories I would take in made me feel bloated and fat.

Putting the nose tube in was one of the worst tasks I've ever done. My dad cringed just watching it happen. The tube burned my throat as the nurse pushed further and further down. I was left struggling to swallow when it was completely inserted. It felt as though something was caught in my throat and immediately my nose began to itch. It was an uncomfortable feeling but the nurses assured me that I would grow used to it.

Then someone came in to take my food order for the following morning's breakfast. I was confused at first because I was sure that before arriving I was told I would have no say over what I ate during my stay. I figured the nurse was making a mistake but I decided to take advantage of it. I ordered my food, staying away from meat and fats. It shocked me that there were five different parts of the breakfast. It also shocked me that I still had to eat during the day even though I was being force-fed throughout the night. I tried to forget about it as I laid back and turned on the TV. But there was nothing good on and I couldn't focus, too much was going on. There was noise everywhere, inside my head and out.

I was still wearing my clothes from school that day. The shorts were extremely uncomfortable and I desperately pined for some comfy sweats. We called my grandparents, who were staying back at home with my brother, and they promised to bring some right away. Along with the sweats they also brought necessities such as toothbrushes, my hairbrush, and clean underwear. I was anxious to receive these items but I dreaded my grandma's arrival. I was mortified by the thought of her seeing me like that. I was a mess. I was ghostly white, completely skin and bones, had a tube down my nose, and my eyes were puffy from crying so much. My health was even worse than my appearance. I had been put in the hospital because of an extremely low heart rate and an unusually cold body temperature. In fact, my body temperature that day was so low that it didn't even show up on the charts that hung on the hospital walls.

My grandma's visit was brief because we were both too tired and distraught to talk. After promising to visit again, she left around eleven o'clock. As soon as she was gone, I tried to settle in and get some sleep. But the sleep was short-lived. An hour later nurses interrupted my rest. They had a patient whose sickness was contagious. For that reason, she needed a private room. She needed my private room. They were sorry but I had to move. Before I had a chance to get up, they were wheeling me down the hall while I still lay shocked in my bed. My parents ran behind me after quickly gathering up our belongings and vacating the first room. I closed my eyes trying to block out the chaos around me. When I opened them again the nurses were wheeling me into another room. This one was shared and only had a single white curtain that divided the two units. My unit was small, and we were crammed together. The nurse stood by while I got myself adjusted, waiting to restart the feeder. She warned us that the fluid would run out every four hours causing it to beep, which would remind the nurse to come refill it.

Suddenly, I was shaken out of my memories and into the present. The nurse had arrived to stop the beeping that had woken me up for the second time during that first hospital night. But this time, she carried a box of supplies. She explained that it was 6:00 a.m., time for her to take my vitals. My temperature, my blood pressure—all of it was written down like some factual statistic. And then she pulled out the needle. I winced because, up until that moment, needles had always been my biggest fear. I cried every time I got my blood taken, no matter what. But somehow, sitting in that hospital bed with the knowledge that if I wasn't there I might die, that needle didn't seem so scary. It was nothing compared to the traumatic experience that had unfolded in the past twenty-four hours. I let the needle prick me without shedding a single tear. It was the first blood test of my visit but I would soon learn that it was not my last. In fact, my blood was taken every morning; I was a blood-taking pro by the time I was released.

Around seven o'clock, the feeding machine was switched off. Around eight o'clock, breakfast arrived. Only something was wrong. The breakfast thrown in front of me looked nothing like what I had ordered. There were three different cartons of "milkshakes" plus a plate of food consisting of bacon, pancakes, and an egg. It didn't even resemble my selections of the night before. And worse, it included meat. But that wasn't all; I also had to eat it all within a half an hour. My parents weren't allowed to be in the room, and a nurse sat by me to supervise and time my meal. A nurse I knew nothing about and who knew nothing about me was my only source of support. And as if things weren't bad enough, the nurse told me that whatever I couldn't eat in the allotted time span I would have to make up for by drinking a food supplement called Ensure. The amount of the supplement would depend on the amount of food left on my plate.

The replacement seemed like an easy alternative; but I soon learned that Ensure tasted like throw-up and drinking it was not the simple solution I had hoped for. Besides, my goal was to leave the hospital as soon as possible, and to do that, I had to show the doctors that I was trying. I had to show them that I was making an effort. So each meal was a mini-challenge. I tried to eat as much as I could, minus the meats, in an attempt to be rid of the supplement. But eating was hard, especially because of the knowledge that I'd also be pumped with calories later that night. I couldn't even exercise to burn off some calories. I was strictly on bed rest. If I wanted to leave my hospital room, I couldn't even walk. Instead, they brought me a wheelchair and pushed me around the building.

That first day was the worst. I anticipated what would happen next and my doctors and physiologists constantly visited me. I was unable to shower because I was connected to the feeding machine, and it took me five minutes just to wheel my way to the bathroom. To my disgust, I was forced to pee in a provided container each time I went so that the nurses could collect and examine it. How disgusting. How depressing. The whole situation at the hospital could be summed up by those two words. Those two words—along with boredom, fat, and tired—became the soundtrack of the next five days.

It was the worst week of my life and the most excruciating task I have ever faced. I missed my dog. I missed my brother. I missed the sunshine outside. I missed my friends. I missed the food we had at home. I missed clean clothes and shampoo. Basically, I missed everything. The hospital was torturous, but at least I thought, I'd be out soon. I kept thinking about Dr. Silber's promise that I'd only have to stay two or three days as long as everything went well. That was my motivation. That was what I wanted. And the fact that I had completely finished almost every meal on that first day and the praise I then received from the doctors around me made me believe that my goal was attainable. But that night, when I asked about discharge, my hopes were quickly shattered and brushed away. Apparently, I was doing so well in the hospital they didn't want to stop it too soon. "But don't worry," they said, "you'll be out by Monday." Monday? But, it was already Tuesday.

Fish Sticks

Okay, so overall the hospital was my absolute lowest point. There are so many words that conjure up chilling memories from that dreadful week. So many words remind me of the discomfort, struggle, pain, and fear. There are the words that you would expect: machine, tube, and sick. But the words that always seem to upset me the most are ones that no one would guess. The words that scare me and remind me of the hospital are "fish sticks."

I'm already terrified at the thought of food. Food only made me feel fat. It made me feel powerless and worthless and guilty. To say it simply: I think food sucks. But no food sucks as much as hospital food. As if eating wasn't hard enough, they served me some of the most disgusting meals I've ever tasted. If you ever find yourself in a hospital, here's a tip: never, I repeat never, eat the scrambled eggs. They're runny and rubbery at the same time. I would bet loads of money that whatever that was they called scrambled eggs was, in fact, not made of eggs. Then there's the pizza. The cheese is rubbery and it's layered with a coating of grease. The crust is like a brick and the sauce smells funny. There's also outdated milk cartons, inedible grilled cheese sandwiches, and chunky bowls of oatmeal. But, by far the worst food I have ever tasted was the hospital's fish sticks. I don't like fish sticks to begin with but those fish sticks scared me for life. They were greasy and burnt and contained about 1% actual fish. It took me the whole half hour just to eat those nasty things. Needless to say, I had to consume a lot of the food supplement after that meal. And I brushed my teeth about ten times that day just to get the disgusting taste to disappear. I never want to see fish sticks placed on a table in front of me again. I'm not sure I could handle it.

But the nasty food wasn't the only miserable part of the hospital. Actually, the whole stint was unbearable. I don't think I've been that bored in my entire life. I was all but tied down to a bed 24/7. There was a TV on the wall but it was daytime during the week and the only shows to watch were either about news or babies. A person can sit around reading or listening to music for only so long before going crazy. I was sick of it all by the second day. My biggest source of excitement was going down a level to get a bone scan taken. They needed to evaluate my bones and determine if I had developed osteoporosis. I changed into a gown and was strapped down on a cold, hard table. A machine took pictures of my body and that was it. That was my big excitement of the week. Then they wheeled me back up to the room, where I continued to sit around, hating life.

Hating life was not an understatement. I told my parents I'd rather be dead. But I also told them that this was going to be a turning point. I finally realized I had a problem. I felt as though I had hit rock bottom. Hopefully, my mom insisted, there was no other way to go now but up. Hopefully, this would be the start of a long line of progress. That is, if I made it through. I literally felt as though I was going to be stuck in that hospital forever. Each day started with hope and ended with disappointment. Each day the doctors told me that everything was going great...but...they were keeping me another day. That's what they said every day. It finally got to a point where I stopped believing them. It finally got to a point where I was about to give up.

And I couldn't stop thinking about school. I knew I was missing the entire week and I wondered if anyone would even notice. I wondered how much people knew and what they were saying. I also felt overwhelmed thinking about all the schoolwork I was missing and how much I would have to make up. Luckily, I wasn't completely out of the school loop because Meredith came to visit me twice. She was supportive the entire time. She called me every night and brought me gifts such as coloring books and finger paints. Two of my other close friends visited too. They made me cards and magazines. It meant a lot to me to know that at least a couple of people cared. They kept me updated on the latest gossip and brought me some of my homework so that I could catch up. Their visits were the highlights of my week. They were brief but they meant the world to me. I had been starting to feel as though no one cared. I had heard about all of the mean comments my old friends were making about my stay, and I felt unloved. Visits from my friends, brother, and grandparents reminded me that I wasn't completely alone.

Then there were all the annoying aspects of the hospital. The most aggravating was the nose tube. Just like the nurses had told me on that first night, I got used to the discomfort. But I still had to deal with the issue of my runny nose. By the third day, I was in desperate need to blow my nose, but doing that with a tube in is nearly impossible. I sniffled vigorously every five minutes. And I rubbed my nose continuously in an attempt to dispel the ongoing itch. There was also the lack of sleep. Every night the machine started its high-pitched squealing as it ran out of fluid. Every morning I awoke to get my vitals taken and every night I fell asleep to the cries of the sick patients in the rooms next door. The atmosphere was anything but ideal. My parents didn't even have a real mattress. They alternated sleeping with me each night. Whoever it was had to endure a night on a cot or couch. By the time the week was over, we must've looked like raccoons with the huge rings that circled under our eyes.

I also had to fight back tears each time I received a phone call or text. Everyone was asking if I was okay and if the rumors were true. I couldn't even give them an answer because at that point I had no idea what the rumors even were. All I knew was that I couldn't hide my secret any longer. I felt exposed and angry. Desperately, I wished that people would understand. I knew they were bound to judge me and I hated them for it. I hated everyone. I hated myself. I hated the hospital. I hated life.

I was admitted into the hospital on a Monday night. I was released on Friday night. The time in between will burn in my memory forever. It was a distraught week. It was a devastating experience. It shook me into the acceptance of my eating disorder and jump-started us onto the road of recovery. I felt nothing but excitement when I was finally released. I was excited to go outside. I was excited to sleep in my own bed. I was excited to take a shower. I was excited to take the tube out and blow my nose. Yes, I was even excited to return to school. But the agony was far from over. In fact, the real journey was just beginning. It was time for me to face this disease head-on. It was time for me to step up to the plate and beat my anorexia once and for all. But doing so would take months. Actually, it might even take years. All I know is that to this day, I am still trying to win against it. And to this day, the memory of the hospital makes me cry and encourages me to keep pushing along. I will never let myself go back there. I will never let myself endure a week like that ever again.

Return

Returning home from the hospital was nothing like what I had imagined. I thought it would be the end of torture but I soon learned it was just going to be a different kind of torture. And although I could finally take that nose tube out during the day, I still had to put it back in every night. The doctors at the hospital made my parents buy a feeding machine and a mass storage of the food supplement so that I could continue the nighttime feedings once I returned home. I was angry and annoyed by it. No one had mentioned that part of the deal when I first entered the hospital. No one told me I'd have to keep it up.

But I guess, in a way, I was a bit lucky. Most anorexics who take a feeding machine home still have to wear the nose tube all day. At the clinic I often saw girls walking in and out with that tube and tape, looking bitter and scared. That's how I would have been if I wasn't brave enough to take the tube in and out by myself. Most girls can't do that because the inserting and ejecting of the tube burns and is painful. But for me, the temporary pain was worth it in order to be tube-free when I went out in public. After all, I was planning to go back to school the following week. I would be mortified if my classmates saw me like that.

By the end of the first two days, it was clear that adjusting to life would be difficult. Not only did we have to deal with the nose tube each night, we also had to set the rate for the machine and continuously refill it with more of the fluid. We had a room full of food supplements that cluttered up our space. We had to deal with those struggles at night and the struggles of regular food during the day. My parents were already desperately trying to get me to eat. We did our best to follow the meal plan and keep up the "thirty-minute meal" rule. But despite our attempts, most meals lasted at least an hour—sixty minutes of pure agony.

The meals were especially hard at first because my mom had not yet adjusted to the many rules my eating disorder had set for me. She didn't know what my scariest foods were so she'd often try to feed me something I wasn't ready to handle. I vividly remember the time that my mom tried to feed me my grandma's homemade lasagna. She wasn't aware that cheese was a terrifying food in my mind, let alone a food that's packed with three types of cheese. Carbohydrates made anything with pasta a big fear too. And what made lasagna the scariest was that it was my former favorite food. I used to beg my grandma for her homemade lasagna and when I was younger I even helped her make it. It used to be a special treat, but when the eating disorder presented itself lasagna became a deadly sin. I don't think I've ever screamed as much or as loud as I did during that particular dinner.

The hardest aspect of my return was getting readjusted to school. It was extra-tricky because I had missed one of the early weeks and I didn't know many people. But the worst part was learning to focus. My life was going up in flames and I was supposed to sit back and learn about how to plot a shape on a graph. All I could think about during class was how scary the past few weeks had been and how difficult life would be in the future. I obsessed over calories and food instead of listening to the teacher. I analyzed the past few months instead of analyzing the book we were told to read in English class. And I had to face rumors. There were lots of rumors that were, for the most part, not true. Apparently, I had fainted in a history class? Okay, sure. That was the craziest lie I'd ever heard. It made me wonder where people came up with stuff because nothing happened that was even remotely similar. I also heard that I had thrown up my intestines. Not true. Everywhere I went, people talked and stared. They judged me and they judged my life. They talked about me as if they knew. They talked as if they understood. But they were all wrong. They didn't know the first thing about the truth of anorexia. They didn't know what it was like or how I felt. And they most definitely did not understand.

Life sucked. Recovery sucked. School sucked. I sucked and people sucked. I had thought that the hospital was as bad as it got. Maybe life right after the hospital wasn't quite as bad, but it wasn't a big improvement either. I cried morning, noon, and night. I told my parents that I hated my life. I begged them to move to Colorado. I wanted to be as far away from my problems, and the rumors, and my current life as I possibly could. This was supposed to be a good year. I was a freshman; it was my start at high school. Isn't there that saying "the high school years are the best years of your life?" Well if that's true, then I didn't even want to imagine how crappy the rest of my life would be.

I feel like I missed out on the first half of that school year. I didn't care about friends or schoolwork or anything besides the anorexia. Recovery took over my life, and not in a positive way. Nothing could be worse than the hospital, but adjusting to life right after it came in a close second. Others my age were going to parties and hanging out with friends. I was sleeping with a nose tube every night and facing my fear of food every day. No one could possibly understand how miserable my life was. I was left alone and felt misunderstood.

Boost

A couple of months after the hospital stay, I got my second ultimatum. To understand what the ultimatum was for, I have to take you back a few months.

The nighttime feeding at home was supposed to be temporary. The goal was to slowly decrease the amount of fluid I took by adding calories throughout the day. The additional calories I needed to eat were like having two good-sized desserts every day. I was not capable of doing that for a long time. At that point, I was barely strong enough to eat breakfast, lunch, and dinner. But even though I couldn't add in meals, getting off the nose tube remained our family's largest goal. There was only one way it could happen without me adding in a lot more food. The doctors told us about a food supplement called Boost. It's a high-calorie drink that many serious athletes take. They recommended that I drink one of these a day to start with. But the task was not as easy as it sounded. Knowing that I was downing a high-calorie drink in the middle of meals was excruciating. It quickly became my most dreaded part of the day. I didn't even like the taste and drinking it just seemed unnecessary to me. Didn't they understand how much more food I was eating already compared to what I had been eating before? Why wasn't that enough for them? But despite my remarks, I was ordered to drink the Boost if I wanted to stop dealing with the nose tube.

After a few weeks of enduring the guilt, pain, and horror of drinking the Boost, we were finally given the okay to stop my nighttime feedings. It was exciting to know that part was over, but the addition of the Boost to my eating regimen made our house a war zone.

Over time, Dr. Silber made it clear that he was not satisfied. He expressed his regret as he explained that something was not working right. Unfortunately, I was not gaining weight fast enough and the Boost was not doing its job. Then he gave me the second ultimatum.

"I'm sorry, but you need to add a second Boost at nighttime. Its either, start drinking two Boosts a day or else we need to readmit you into the hospital." His words sucked out all of my hope and happiness. I felt the ground begin to shake and the walls around me start to spin. I screamed through deep sobs. I chanted "NO" over and over. I shook violently. I couldn't see. My eyes were blurred with tears. I didn't have enough power to drink two Boosts a day. I could barely manage one. This couldn't be happening. I had promised myself that I'd never go into the hospital again. I had promised myself I would never let that happen. But what could I do? I couldn't drink two Boosts. I just couldn't. The idea seemed disastrous. When I locked eyes with my mom, I knew she was thinking the same thing. How could our family manage twice the anguish? I thought about my options but the only one that sounded doable to me was dying. Death would be way easier than either of the options I was just given. That's how scared I was. I was so scared that death became appealing. I was so scared that life seemed impossible to live.

I kept repeating this again and again. "I just want to die, I just want to die." As I spoke, the people around me were staring back with sympathy. Dr. Silber was obviously worried. Anyone would be if they witnessed someone falling apart like I was. I begged him for other options. He told us that there was only one more. He told us that my parents could admit me into a treatment facility. I would miss many weeks of school and live away from my family. It seemed disastrous but yet, it was my best option so far. But getting admitted into a facility would take time. I couldn't go in to one that night. I had to go home first. I had to go home and try my best. The following day I would go down to Children's National Medical Center in Washington, DC and meet with Dr. Silber again.

I don't know how I got through that night, but I did because before I knew it, my mom was picking me up from school and telling me it was time to eat lunch. It was a normal routine for us, but I just couldn't do it. The moment I saw the food in front of me, all I could think of was the horrible experience of the night before and all the food that was to come my way once I entered the facility. I refused to eat. I didn't even respond to my mom's normal threats to take me to the hospital. I just sat emotionless, refusing to eat. My eating disorder had full control over me. There was nothing my mom could do.

When we arrived at the hospital, Dr. Silber's assistant told us that I needed to eat lunch. But still, I refused. Just like there was nothing my mom could do, there was nothing that lady could do either. But she insisted that I try. She sent us down to the hospital cafeteria and ordered my mom to find me a reasonable lunch. If I could eat it then I wouldn't have to go back to the hospital immediately. I could go home and wait for my acceptance to the eating disorder treatment center instead. So my mom dragged me downstairs and set the tray in front of me—a plate of rice, fish, and disgusting green beans. It was a full plate. It was a scary plate. It reminded me of all the plates

I received in the hospital bed not too long ago. And I was in the hospital. The smell, the scenery, the taste of the food; it was all too familiar. As the memories overtook me, I stood up and pushed the tray away with force. As the rice spilled onto the table, I sprinted away. I ran out of that room full of people with tears stinging my eyes. I ran past the waiting rooms and the doctors and the nurses. I didn't know where I was going but I knew that I needed to get away. I needed to leave the memories. I needed to escape the food. I needed to be free of all my difficult choices. I found a safe little corner where I curled up and cried.

After fifteen minutes, I realized that my mom was probably worrying about me. I had left her in the cafeteria. I felt ashamed and guilty but also angry that she would put me in such a situation in the first place. I started to head back toward her, but I turned around after taking a few steps. I couldn't just walk back in as if nothing had happened. It was all so embarrassing. I didn't know what to do. I needed my mom. I needed a hug. But if I went back she'd be angry and yell at me. I knew they would readmit me to the hospital now. I felt like a failure.

The next few hours were a blur. I don't know how, but I managed to return home. It was my dad's birthday. I begged the doctors to give him a gift and let me go back and see him. I begged them to give me another chance. I promised I'd do better. I promised I'd do whatever it took to stay as far away from the hospital as possible. And somehow, by a miracle, I was given what I asked for. And when they accepted my promises, I knew I couldn't let them down.

The next few weeks I pushed myself farther than I ever had before. I did everything I was told although I still had to scream and cry as I did it. In the meantime, my parents researched different treatment centers and we kept the idea of going to one in the back of our minds. I was just days away from being sent to one. I was just days away from leaving school and leaving my home. But, I never went. The reminder of how much I hated the hospital had fueled me to dig down for more strength. I realized that going to a facility would be even worse than going back in the hospital. I realized how hard it would be to leave my family and friends. I realized how weak I would feel if I let that happen. I needed to prove to everyone that I was brave. I needed to prove to myself that I was strong.

There were times when I wished I could be in a treatment place. I wished things were easier and that I didn't have to do so much work myself. There were times I wished I could leave school and escape the drama and pressure. But overall, I know that I am lucky to have avoided it.

I know there were times when my parents wished that I was in a treatment center. They wished they didn't have to deal with all of my breakdowns and tantrums. Sometimes they were scared of the person I became when my eating disorder had control. Sometimes they feared I would hurt them or hurt myself. They wished it were easier. But overall, they know that I am lucky to have avoided it.

Recovery was anything but easy after that and my problems didn't disappear. But I still felt proud when I thought of how close I was to taking things to a whole new level. I felt proud when I thought of the drive that kept me from falling even deeper into the depths of my controlling eating disorder.

Routine

Recovery was in full swing. A monotonous routine was established and life as I knew it was long gone. In its place was a chaotic, depressed, and stressful version of the world. Every day began with tears and ended with thoughts of death. It was a struggle for me to get through each hour, to continue on and fight for my life. The schedule was always the same. It went exactly like this:

5:30 a.m. - Wake up and sneak into the next room to do sit-ups. I did hundreds a day in an attempt to gain only muscle and no fat.

6:00 a.m. - After ten minutes of fear while my meal was being prepared, I would come down and eat, crying as I did so.

6:30 a.m. - I'd look for the best outfit I could find. Sure, I felt horrible, but that didn't mean I had to look horrible too. However, despite my best efforts and cutest clothes, I left the house feeling ugly and unimportant as usual.

7:30 until 10:00 a.m. - I sat through my morning classes, barely speaking a word to anyone, barely even paying attention. Although I tried to focus, my thoughts continuously drifted back to food. In addition, I would constantly compare myself to the other girls around me while wondering what size jeans they wore and what they had eaten so far that day.

10:00 a.m. - It was my lunch period but I didn't go to lunch. It was the period to hang out and socialize with my friends, but I didn't converse with anyone. I walked up the stairs and took numerous laps around the entire school. It was my only opportunity to exercise. Every so often, after walking past a classroom three or four times I'd blush as a student in the front row stared at me quizzically. But I'd shake off the embarrassment and continue on, desperate to burn some calories.

10:30 a.m. - Lunch was still in progress, but I was still alone. Shortly, my mom would come to take me home for snack. When she arrived, I piled in her car and exploded with complaints about another horrible day. Following that, I screamed and cried and fought, finally managing to eat and drink all that was necessary.

11:00 a.m. - I returned to school and dried up my tears as I walked to fifth period, which was gym; as usual, I didn't change. I couldn't participate and by then my classmates had given up on finding out the reason why. It was a good thing considering I had given up on thinking of a believable excuse.

12:00 until 2:00 p.m. - I dragged my way through afternoon classes. The day went on as it had in the morning. The teachers would talk but all I would hear were my thoughts on what I'd have to eat next. The only good part of the day came around 1:00 p.m. I had that period with Meredith, the only friend who seemed to be sticking with me through my issues.

2:30 p.m. - Once home, I would have to eat lunch. Each lunch started off with more screaming, more crying, and sometimes even throwing. I lost control as I angrily swiped all the paper off the island and threw myself on the ground, covering them all up. Even worse, I had started a new way to release my emotions. The anger from food welled up so much that I felt as though I might punch someone. To avoid this, I clenched my nails into my opposite arm and tried to squeeze out all of my pain. After a while, this began leaving marks and I had to stop.

3:00 until 7:00 p.m. - I began to fear dinner. I lay around the house worrying, desperately trying to conjure a way to get out of it. I went to my room, worried, and cried. I went downstairs, worried, and cried. I went to my mom, worried, and cried. I stepped on the back porch, worried, and cried. If you haven't noticed, basically all I did during those long afternoons was worry and cry.

7:30 p.m. - Dinner finally came. Most of the time the meal was a surprise and I never quite knew what it was going to be. However, occasionally I would smell a certain food ahead of time and obsess over what that smell could be until I came up with an answer. On those days, dinner was even harder. When I knew about the meal beforehand it gave my eating disorder more time to convince me that I absolutely could not eat it. The longer I knew, the more dangerous the food would seem. But whether I knew in advance or not, dinner was always the hardest meal. It was hardest because it was never the same. Unlike breakfast, snack, and lunch, dinner was always changing. New foods were constantly introduced and each one seemed scarier than the last. I would come downstairs and begin to scream, no matter what food was put in front of me. I lost all control and began running in circles around the room. Every five circles I would let out another deafening scream. I would cry and shake the whole way through the meal. I'd gasp for breath and yell at my parents. I hated them. I hated them for doing this to me. I hated them for making me eat. I hated them; and, most of all, I hated food.

8:30 p.m. - Dinner would finally end and I would beg and plead to go for a short walk. I'd start to worry about eating for the next day and pray that the eating for the current day was over.

9:00 p.m. - I'd go to sleep early, tired from the emotionally draining saga of events. I was weak and worn down. My parents were just as tired from witnessing the multiple outbursts as I was from having them. I would end the day with an apology. The regret I felt for my behavior was infinite. But each time, they would gently remind me what the doctor said. Nothing I did was my fault, and I could not be held responsible for my actions.

That was it. That was how each day was spent. That was how semester one of my freshman year panned out. That was recovery. The only time the schedule changed was when I had another appointment, which seemed to be every other day. As time went on, the appointments I had to schedule piled up. Eventually, I had to go to four therapy sessions a week. There were two individual therapy sessions, one family therapy session, and one group therapy session. On top of that, each week I had either a doctor's appointment or a psychiatrist appointment. The clinic in Spring Valley that had once seemed so foreign and unknown was now my second home. We went there so many times a week that my mom would joke, "By now the car could drive there all by itself!"

In between all the worrying and therapy, I did my best to make time for schoolwork. I was behind because of the many missed classes from my stay in the hospital as well as from my early dismissals. Still, I pushed myself the best I could, managing to get A's and B's the first quarter and straight A's the second. But it didn't matter. None of it mattered. School, friends, fun—the words were meaningless. The focus of my life was recovery and each day was just as painful as the last. I spent each day wishing I were dead. I spent each day losing myself to the eating disorder. This was it. This was my life as a recovering anorexic.

Betrayal

A celebrity picks up a magazine. Inside she finds herself on the "Worst Dressed" list. For a second she feels upset. But she assures herself she'll make it on the "Best Dressed" list the following week. And that's the end of it. She moves on with her luxurious life.

An old woman drives down a winding road. She's in search of 7081 Candy Drive. She was supposed to be at the house an hour ago. Her daughter would halt the feast in hopes that her mother was just around the corner. But the woman is lost. She frantically looks over her directions, unable to place where she is. She asks a pedestrian for help. He claims he's in a hurry and apologizes as he runs across the street. The woman finds it a bit rude but she just turns the other way to look for someone else. And that's the end of it. She moves on with her quest.

A football team hears the quarterback of their rival school talking smack. The quarterback claims that the team "plays like a group of girls" and that his "grandma could play better" than them. The team gets angry for a split second, embarrassed by the remarks. But they decide to let it go and get their revenge by beating the rival school in next week's game. And that's the end of it. They move on with their intense training.

When let down by strangers, by insignificant observers, or by distant acquaintances, it is easy to make a quick recovery. You don't know them. They don't know you. Their opinion means nothing. What they say or do may have a slight effect but that is as far as the sadness will go. It's not a betrayal. No, it's just a slight setback, a petty insult. To have betrayal you need to have trust. To have betrayal you need to have love.

A girl feels happiness with her boyfriend. He treats her like she's the most important girl in the world. He can always make her smile, and they share a connection that cannot be denied. That is, until he cheats on her. The realization of what he has done hits hard. Her heart begins to ache, and she feels a deep sob building up inside of her. Running to her room she lets out a sigh. Tears pour out like water from a spring. His compliments and his claims of love—were they all just a lie? She's not good enough. She's never good enough.

A friend tells the girl she's ugly. She's too skinny and looks disgusting. She feels a knife carve its way into her back. It surprises her when she reaches behind to pull it out and there's nothing there. She feels her face burn red with embarrassment. The next day she looks in the mirror and echoes of her friend's voice ring through her ears. She begins to speak softly to herself saying, "You're ugly. You're gross. You're disgusting. You're nothing." With each whispered word the more the girl believes. From then on she feels her confidence drop with every interaction between her and that friend.

The girl is in a hospital bed clinging onto her life. But where are her best friends? A couple of friends come to show support, but the ones she felt closest to don't show up. In fact, when they receive the news of her hospitalization they spread it around the whole school. Even worse, they are heard making comments such as "She deserves it" and "It's her own fault." The girl once called them her best friends but now, in desperate need of their support, they turn their backs on her. They mock her. She cries herself to sleep that night. In the days that follow, she constantly asks herself what she did wrong. Why don't they like her anymore? Is she that horrible of a person? They turn their backs on her, yet she places the blame on her own shoulders.

Betrayal sneaks into the souls of those we rely on the most. It doesn't come from strangers. It doesn't come from rivals. Betrayal comes from friends, family, and people we love. To feel betrayed is the worst feeling possible.

The more you trust someone the more power they have to hurt you. With each secret you tell them the more information they have to potentially use against you. With each dream you share the more ideas they have to crush your hopes. The more love you give them the more hate they can give back.

Why is it that betrayal is felt so strongly from those we know the best? Is it because they mean something to us? We know about them. We know their dislikes and their likes. We know their past and their present. We wanted to be a part of their future. So when they let us down and fill us with upsetting memories, it hurts all the more because we know we once shared happiness together.

Is it because we relied on them? They are the people we count on to pick us up when we're down. They are the people who could make us laugh when we wanted to cry. But after their betrayal the tables have turned. Suddenly, they are the ones knocking us down so there's no one to pick us up. They are the ones making us cry so there's no one to make us laugh. They brought us happiness, but suddenly, the thought of them brings us pain.

Or perhaps it is a combination of both? No matter the reason, one thing is for sure. When betrayed by someone close, a permanent scar is left on your heart. The betrayal is a constant reminder that people are not always what they seem and the only person you can trust is yourself.

Victory

The next battle was looming in the air around me. I could sense it coming on. I tried desperately to shut it down, but the arrival was ominous. I had to prepare for war.

I got my ammo ready: the thoughts of success, the hope of freedom, the motivation of a normal life. I was ready to use these weapons to fight. Unfortunately, the enemy was pulling out weapons of its own. You're stupid, you're fat, you're ugly and worthless, you have no control, no power. These weapons were strong, even deadly if used at the right time. It would be a grand battle of strength and bravery. I wasn't sure if I could make it, but I had to try.

I made my way down the stairs, my heart beating rapidly, my palms beginning to sweat. I looked at the faces around me, all of them unaware of how tough the battle would be to win. I took a deep breath and sat down. My legs and arms began to shake like an earthquake. As I stared down at the food, the enemy began to fire. The tears began rolling down my face like a waterfall as I struggled to stand strong against the bullets being shot at me. It seemed as if I was no match for the enemy. My weapons began drifting farther and farther away as the bullets hit me harder and harder. A feeling of discouragement and hopelessness welled up inside of me, and I let out a scream.

I desperately grabbed for my weapons and used all my might to fire back. I took a bite. Then another. I slowly began to regain strength. But the enemy wasn't giving up yet.

"You're horrible!" It screamed as it reloaded and fired rapidly one more time. As I continued to eat, it continued to shoot. I hung on to my strength by a thread, just praying it would be over soon. Then finally, the food was gone. I had won the battle. It had taken everything in me, but I had done it.

Yet even though the battle ended, the war was far from over. I had to regain my strength for the next battle.

Movement

Movement. No matter what, I always needed to move. Recovery was underway, and I had recently bumped up my calorie intake in an attempt to phase off of the Boost. But, the doctors had taken away movement; I wasn't allowed to exercise. The weight gain was inevitable, and deep down I knew that was for the best.

But an agonizing feeling hovered over me as this realization came crashing down. Somehow I had to prevent it. I needed to gain the weight. I needed to avoid gaining the weight. I needed to take in the calories. I needed to run away from the calories. My mind began an internal battle that still lasts to this day. I couldn't think straight, but one thing felt clear—I needed movement. Any chance I got to move I took it. Even burning one extra calorie by walking from here to there would make me content. No, I couldn't get away from consuming the calories. But maybe I could get rid of them. I knew the idea was destructive. I knew I'd gain weight anyway. But any effort I could make to gain back some pride could not be turned away.

It became a necessity. If I wasn't moving, if I wasn't distracting myself, all I would do was worry. I'd just sit there worrying about the next meal and the last. I couldn't spend my day like that. So, I needed to move.

The toughest time of day to find this movement was the early mornings. On the weekends, I'd wake up at 6:30 a.m., eat my breakfast, and then start worrying. I couldn't go back to sleep. I had too much guilt for that, too much on my mind. At first, my parents took me for short walks around the block. When we needed to run an errand at stores like Home Depot or the bank, we'd tackle that instead. But no matter what the case, I always needed movement.

As the weather turned from crisp and cool to chilled and icy, the morning walks became a dilemma. We tried to continue them at first but our fingers would turn blue from the cold and our mouths were too numb to talk. The biggest problem for me was the freezing I felt in my nose. In my opinion, someone should invent a nose warmer. There's a special accessory to keep practically every other body part warm, but there's still nothing for the nose. The cold nose was just too much. Even

I had to admit that continuing our walks would be nothing short of insanity.

"The mall!" my dad exclaimed as we congregated to brainstorm a substitution, "What about the mall?" Good question. What about the mall? What could the mall possibly have to do with anything right now? *Pretty random,* I thought, but then I knew it was the answer.

"The mall is always open early, even though the stores are still closed. Elderly people go there to get exercise or something. We could try going to the mall." And so it was decided. The next morning I trotted into the empty mall with my dad following close behind.

I've been to the mall thousands of times. Smells of food and perfumes fill the air. People walk purposefully in every direction. Sales people seem to appear at every corner. Lights flood out of every room. Nothing can be heard besides the noisy chatter of the customers as they gab to their friends. Yes, I knew all about the mall. You might even say I knew it like the back of my hand. But standing here, looking around, at 7:00 a.m. on a Sunday morning, I felt as though I was seeing the mall for the first time.

This was not the place I knew and loved. This was not "the back of my hand." The only smell that filled the air was that of the various cleaning products. There were hardly any people besides the occasional little, old lady who walked at a snail's pace. Salespeople were nowhere in sight, and each store was flooded with darkness. The only sounds were the sniffles from the aged man to my left and the coughing from the lady to my right. I looked at my dad, and we began to walk.

Entering the main area, a new sound rang out from above. It was music. Not current music by any means, but it was music. My dad quickly named the song, telling me his parents used to listen to it when he was little. It was music from back before he was even born. It was music for the few people that wandered these empty halls. Each old-timer we passed seemed to be singing softly to herself. Personally, I thought it was horrible, but I guess I wasn't the type of person the music was geared to. So I tried my best to tune it out and continued along on my walk.

"Dad, watch out!" I pulled him out of the way as some lady in her sixties hightailed it past us. She was wearing a tracksuit and had a water bottle attached at her hip. For a second, I found this a bit odd. But over the next few months, I learned that this was the usual with the early mall-goers.

Another week we were walking along lazily, enjoying our time, when out of nowhere, two elderly couples lapped us twice. The idea that these four people could lap us made me laugh. They looked as though they were about to fall over. They wore hearing aids and hunched over as they walked.

One week we even saw an old lady with a walker scooting her way across the mall. That same day I witnessed three eyebrow-raising workout routines. The first was an aged Asian lady who paced up and down the stairs for at least a half an hour. The second was a man sprawled out on the floor with his legs stretched out in front of him; he was reaching desperately for his toes. The third was by far the funniest. A lady threw her hands against the wall in front of her and pushed backwards. Her butt stuck out and she wriggled it left to right as if showing it off to the world. I covered my mouth and stifled a giggle, trying not to be heard. What made it even funnier was the pair of bright pink pants she wore with a neon blue jacket. *Oh wow*, I thought to myself with amusement, *it's a living cotton candy.* I looked back at her and laughed harder. She was beginning to hum, loudly and not at all to herself. Her eyes were closed and she picked up the pace of her butt wriggling. *Ha. She probably forgot she's in public. Some people are just so clueless.*

Although these early mall trips provided me with laughs and entertainment, they weren't exactly ideal. But we continued on with them each weekend because I needed movement. I needed those trips.

Homecoming

Homecoming was on its way and anticipation was bouncing off the walls of our school. Everyone seemed to be talking about their outfits and their dates. Pre-party invitations were passed out and plans were made. Limos were ordered and dinner reservations were set. The social circuit was buzzing, but I planned to watch from the outside. I had no time to work on an event of my own because each day was ruled by my anorexia. I couldn't even buy a new dress in advance because, if all went according to plan, my weight and size would increase by the time I needed to wear it. And I didn't make dinner plans because I was supposed to have all my meals supervised.

To my surprise, I was invited to two pre-parties. One was bigger, more expensive. It included a limo and dinner at a fancy restaurant. The other was more laid-back. I wouldn't even call it a party. Meredith had invited a few people over to her house to get ready and go out to eat. My decision was clear—I'd go to Meredith's. The other party had some guests who I didn't exactly want to see. Besides, homecoming without Meredith wouldn't even matter. She was becoming my best friend, and we promised we'd conquer this new experience together. Our other friend stuck with us too. The three of us decided to get ready alone because of a drama that was circulating around the grade. We didn't want any of it to ruin our evening. We were perfectly content with just each other. There were only two problems.

The first problem was the issue of dates. Both Meredith and our other friend had boyfriends. Their dates were set. But finding me a date was not as easy. Preoccupied with my near-death experience that I had recently survived, I had barely talked to anyone since school started. However, Meredith and our friend put their heads together and made a plan. Apparently, Meredith's boyfriend knew a guy who they claimed was "perfect" for me. Immediately, the boy and I clicked. So the six of us began to hang out. My two friends, me, and the three guys—together we made the perfect group of six. Not to mention the perfect group for homecoming. That is up until a few weeks before homecoming. Meredith and her boyfriend broke up unexpectedly. Our perfect group was no more. After assuring Mere that we wouldn't leave her out, she finally agreed to come despite her worries of becoming a fifth wheel. That problem seemed to be solved.

The second problem was dinner. I still didn't know if I could go. How was I supposed to get my parents to let me eat a meal unsupervised? How was I even supposed to eat in public and act civilized? The idea seemed in possible. I needed a miracle.

Two weeks before the dance, my miracle came. I rolled out of bed only to find, that for the first time in months, I had gotten my period. This was a huge sign to the doctors that my body was regaining its health. The sign was so epic that my dad even began tearing up once I told him. My parents were so happy, so proud, and so hopeful. They reluctantly agreed to give me one night of freedom. For one night I would be normal. For one night I would have fun.

Finally, two days before homecoming, things were falling into place. Our dinner reservations were set, I had a date, and best of all, I had a new dress. My mom even set up an appointment for me to get my hair done. For the first time in a long time, life was looking up.

Then it was here. The day was here. I filled up with excitement as I slipped on my plum colored halter dress. It had a diamond brooch where the dress hit my chest and flowed out at the bottom. I felt like a princess as I marched into the salon to complete my look. All I wanted were some soft curls, just a curly chunk of hair here and there, but nothing too dramatic. In my mind everything was perfect. But reality hit hard as he swiveled my chair around to meet the mirror. I tried not to scream. I tried not to show how I felt. The stylist looked so pleased. He looked as though he had created a masterpiece. But to me it was a nightmare. Big, powerful curls filled my head. It poofed out, making my face seem even fatter. I felt hideous. I looked down at my dress. Suddenly, it too looked hideous. Who was I kidding, thinking I could be pretty for a day? I'll never be pretty. I felt foolish and stupid. I felt miserable.

I moaned my way into Meredith's only to be greeted by a cluster of high-pitched squeals. They loved my hair. Or at least, that's what they said. Secretly though, I wondered if it was all just a lie. How could I know they really loved it? I couldn't, but I thanked them all the same. We giggled and chattered as we waited for the boys to arrive.

A corsage. My date brought me a corsage. It was so cute and unexpected; it was all I could do not to start laughing with embarrassment. A megawatt smile crept across my face. We posed for pictures and for a moment I forgot to think about how ugly I must've looked in them. Everything was going perfectly. I was feeling ten times happier, and I knew that eating a good-sized meal would only ruin that happiness.

We arrived at Mamma Lucia's with hope for the night ahead. Pizza, it was pizza. That's what this restaurant was known for. That's what people would choose to eat. But I knew that was absolutely impossible for me. I had to order a salad. This was my only night of freedom and I felt as though I had to take advantage of it. If I didn't then I would be weak, giving in to my hunger. The temptation to return to my old ways was too strong. I ate two bites of salad with pride. I talked continuously, hoping no one would notice the mound of food still left on my plate. I sipped my diet coke and smiled to myself. The night was going perfectly. Just like that, I was sucked back into the tunnel of threatening lies. Just like that, my eating disorder took back control.

The rest of the night wasn't as good as I had hoped. The gym was hot and crowded. My feet began to ache from my painful shoes. I kept losing sight of Meredith, and the music wasn't all that great either. I hoped the after party would turn the night around. I hoped the after-party would be unforgettable.

But the letdowns kept coming. Drama filled the house as we crept up the hostess's stairs to change out of our dresses. One girl had caught her friend dancing with her ex. Another girl was trying to woo another girl's date. Two boys told another boy that he smelled, right in front of his girlfriend. One girl was constantly fighting with her boyfriend. No matter where I went, there was drama. The night wasn't amazing. The night wasn't perfect. But in the end, I was happy. I had felt the taste of freedom graze my lips. I had experienced my first social extravaganza since being diagnosed. I had enjoyed the company of my two friends. Best of all, I topped the night off with a kiss from my date. For once, nothing was perfect and that was all right with me.

Halloween

For the past two years, Halloween had been a night of letdowns. For the past two years, I had spent my Halloween crying, wondering what was wrong with me and why no one cared. I watched those around me laugh the night away while I sat back and put all my effort into holding a simple smile.

The first time was in eighth grade. I was going trick-or-treating with my three best friends and then back to one of their houses for a sleepover. We spent hours joking around carelessly in the mall as we searched for costumes. We finally settled on the "guy" theme by buying boxers, boy's athletic shorts, baseball hats, and "bling." We talked about it for weeks. I was excited and filled with high hopes. Spending the night with my best friends seemed ideal. How was I to know what was about to come my way?

I'm not quite sure how the fight began. It was over something stupid, I'm sure. But no matter what happened, in the end, I was left alone. Alone, in the dark, in the middle of a strange neighborhood. They were mad at me. I hadn't done anything. Or had I? I stood on the side of the street confused, desperate, and alone. Looking back, I can point out the symbolism. I realized that deserting me that Halloween was a foreshadowing of the future. They left me then and they would leave me during the anorexia. It should have been a warning that they were not friends I could count on. But I didn't think of it like that. Instead, I punished myself. I told myself that, although I couldn't remember anything, I must've done something wrong. I told myself that I deserved to be left and they were right to be mad at me. I couldn't even blame them because I agreed. They were angry with me, and I was angry with myself. It was a turning point on my journey to low self-esteem. A few weeks later we would make up, but the memory of the night remained, leaving me with self-doubt and self-hate.

Fast-forward one year and everything had changed. By Halloween of ninth grade I knew I was anorexic and was struggling to stay alive. Those three best friends from the year before had barely talked to me in the past three months. They joined together with Meredith's old best friends and left us out. They decided to dress up, the six of them, without including us. So then, Meredith and I turned to each other once again. We went shopping to pick out costumes and make plans to attend a Halloween party that night. Beforehand, we decided to do some trick-or-treating with some mutual friends. The idea was slightly scary. At that point in my recovery, collecting candy was torturous. But my mom reminded me that no one would make me eat the candy and with Meredith's pleas, I finally agreed.

Unfortunately, the plan is to go between 6:00 and 9:00 p.m., heading over to the party straight afterward. This just happened to be right smack in the middle of my dinnertime and it seemed as though I wouldn't go after all. I knew I should've been disappointed but all I felt was relief. I didn't enjoy hanging out with girls my age anymore. I'd much rather stay home and obsess over food and calories. But my parents were determined. They saw my lack of social activity and were desperate for me to participate. They found it best for me to spend a night with my friends, to remember what it was like to have fun, and to focus on something besides my eating disorder. So, they devised a plan. They told me I could trick-or-treat with my friends for an hour, come home and eat, then drive over to the party and meet up with them again. Sounded simple enough, right?

But then I realized a problem: what would I do with all the food that would be at the party? Everyone would be pigging out on the sweets and snacks, but I would've already eaten dinner. Could I handle the stress of being around so much food? I wasn't sure, but my parents insisted I had to try. So that night, I went out trick-or-treating with everything going according to plan. We walked and laughed and banged on the doors as we made our way throughout the neighborhood. But the whole time I found my mind constantly wandering back to dinner. I was impulsively checking the time every five minutes. It seemed as though the hour went on forever, until finally, it was 7:00 p.m. I quietly excused myself from the group and headed on my way back home.

And then I let my eating disorder take control. I realized that I was completely on the other side of the neighborhood, at least a good half of a mile from my house. Thoughts of the food I would have to eat and the enormous mound of candy in my bag invaded my mind and caused me to start running. I was sprinting, actually. Sprinting past the young kids with their parents and the many houses decorated with every kind of Halloween prop imaginable. I must've looked like an idiot, but I couldn't have cared less. It didn't matter; I was burning calories and sneaking in exercise. As my house grew near, I began to slow down. I knew I had to calm myself down, steady my breath, and wipe away my sweat before returning home. I stood outside my house for five minutes before finally mustering up the courage to open the door and step into my nightmare. The food was waiting for me. It was sitting on the table and each parent sat on one side of it. They were all waiting. The pressure built up, as always, and caused me to scream. Good thing I remembered to shut the front door on my way inside. Actually, it was a really good thing considering the screams grew more frequent and louder as the meal went on.

An hour and a half later I was mustering up courage outside of a different house. I could hear music coming from inside and knew the party was already in full swing. I entered the house with nerves and feelings of guilt that were still left over from dinner. I cautiously stepped down the stairs praying that Meredith would already be in the room. When I turned the corner and saw her smile at me, I instantly relaxed. She ran up and hugged me, and we began to party. But the disasters of my night were far from over. The same three girls who made my last Halloween hell would make this one even worse. When they arrived, they brushed past us, not even saying a word. Sure we hadn't been as close to them lately, but still, they used to call us their best friends and now it was as if they didn't know we existed. Listening to them reflect on the fun of their pre-party hurt our feelings. We remembered a time when we too were part of their fun. We remembered a time when we too were invited to their houses and sleepovers. They didn't speak one word to us the whole night. Surrounded by a sea of excited people at a party filled with music and games, Mere and I ended up locked in the bathroom, crying on the floor.

I don't remember who initiated it, but one of us dragged the other into the small room in the corner of the basement. We hugged each other beside the toilet and sink. We sobbed and opened up to each other with every complaint and every betrayal. I let out my feelings of pain that came as a result of recovery, and she let out her pain that came as a result of losing her one-time best friend. We both needed a friend. We both needed each other. We didn't leave each other's side the rest of the night. She stood by me while I tried avoiding the food table, and I stood by her while she tried avoiding them. We both felt hurt and confused.

At the end of the night, I thought I had actually gotten away with it. I had eaten nothing, and no one had said a word. No one had asked if I was hungry or why I chose not to eat. No one knew. I had kept it a secret. Or so I thought. Months later I learned that on Halloween the rumors surrounding my anorexia had grown. I didn't know it, but people began to talk. They talked about how skinny I looked and the lack of food I ate. Little did they know, I was already aware, I already knew my issue and what I needed to do to fix it. They didn't know how hard it was or how painful each day proved to be. Not even our old best friends took the time to find this out. That upset me. It upset Meredith. But we had each other. It was another unhappy Halloween, but at least this time, we had each other.

Adjusting

Life at school during the months of recovery was torture. Not only was it torture, it was unfair, tiring, and difficult. I struggled to focus in class daily. How could I possibly learn how to "solve for x" or write an essay when my home life was so disastrous and life threatening? None of the teachings seemed important anymore. The only topics that mattered to me were food, depression, and anorexia. Worst of all, it seemed as though these topics appeared everywhere I went.

Withstanding high school amongst a sea of high-powered, superficial, teenage girls is no easy task. No matter who you're with or why you're there, appearance seems to be foremost in everyone's thoughts. Girls seem to constantly comment on their peers clothes, bodies, and hairstyles. Walking through the halls brings fear and worry because, deep down, we all know we're being judged.

"Doesn't it look like Sandy has put on a few pounds?" The voice next to me whispers innocently into my left ear. "I mean, come on. It's so obvious she needs a bigger pant size. Can you say disgusting?" A giggle escapes the girl's mouth as she turns and walks away. As I stand there, processing the words that were just spoken, I can't help but wonder, *do people say that about me? Do they think I'm disgusting?* My guess is that they do, which makes it ten times harder to eat later that day. Teenage girls are extremely observant and when I sat down to dinner, I was certain that if I ate pasta that night, my classmates would notice it the next day.

Then there's the fact that every discussion between high school girls seems to center around food and weight. Everywhere I go, I can't escape the drones of "I want to lose five pounds" or "I haven't eaten all day." Eating disorder or not, girls will say anything to appear thin in another's eyes. Many girls feel the need to boast about what they've eaten and what they haven't. Each teen feels the need to boast about what they weigh and what they will weigh. Each teen feels the need to be the best.

"Oh my god, I'm SO super hungry! I haven't eaten real food in over twenty-four hours." As she speaks I silently beg her to shut up. I hope that, by some luck, she will decide not to continue on. It is soon obvious that my prayers will not be answered.

"See, 'cause yesterday I was like at Jessie's like all day long and we just nibbled on some chocolate for our dinner. And then this morning I had to wake up for swim practice at like four in the morning so I didn't eat breakfast. Then at lunch, I realized that I totally spaced and forgot mine, yet again."

I tried my hardest to be immune to her words. I tried my hardest to forget them and continue on. But, as much as I wished I didn't, I still had an eating disorder, and ignoring her comments was not a possibility. I immediately remembered what I had eaten over the past day and began to compare. As I added up all the foods that were basically shoved down my throat that morning and the night before, I realized I had eaten almost four times as much as this girl had. To me, that meant I was four times fatter, four times uglier, and four times weaker. I felt suffocated. The world spun as I picked up my pace and sprinted for the nearest hideout. Locking myself in the stall, I let go as the tears fell rapidly down my face. As usual, I couldn't get through the day without hearing about another girl's eating habits and comparing them to my own. As usual, I could not avoid the talks about food and weight. As usual, I wished that I didn't go to school.

But escaping the conversations of girls around me was not the only unbearable part of school. The added struggles appeared when a teacher made an attempt to be giving and nice. That struggle arose when a teacher handed out sweets.

"If you guys are well-behaved with the sub tomorrow, then I'll give you each a surprise when I get back." The history teacher's announcement planted excitement on nearly everyone's face. Mine was the exception. The only emotion that sentence evoked was fear. I feared the surprise. I feared knowing it would be some sort of candy or drink. My fear was not far off. The surprise revealed itself as hot chocolate. The reward was like a punishment. I sat silently, mentally begging people to leave me alone, while I watched those around me drink and laugh and enjoy. A few people ignored my mental pleas and asked me why I wasn't drinking the hot chocolate. With a grunt, I replied that I just didn't like chocolate. They called me crazy and went on with their happiness. I scowled.

"All right, since it's almost Christmas, I brought you some goodies." The science teacher pulled out candy canes and mini chocolate bars. She scurried around the room, placing a small heap of candy on every student's desk. Almost immediately afterward, she handed out the expected unit test and commanded us to begin. I knew the material. I studied the material. I was ready. But I didn't do well. That test was returned with a C and, I knew why. There was just no way that I could concentrate during the test when there was a mound of chocolate taunting me. It was the worst kind of distraction. It was temptation.

Then there were the dreaded times that both these issues were combined. Teachers' generosity met with my fellow girls' food conversations. A small flame erupted into a massive fire. For instance, the time we had to make a cake for our history project. In an attempt to gain our approval, my history teacher gave us the option to construct a cake, instead of a poster, to symbolize the topic we were researching. Food talks began to fill the air when the cakes were brought in that following Friday. All around me girls spoke of how they had saved up for this class and how much cake they were going to allow themselves to eat. Each group presented their cake with pride and diligently carved it into pieces. It was like a party. Everyone was talking and laughing and eating. But I was sitting there alone, holding back my tears. Just being around that many sweets overwhelmed me. Just being around all the people who didn't understand made me feel alone. Yet again, I found myself wishing I didn't go to school.

Those first few months were hard to get through. Somehow, I stuck around and made it through freshman year. I stayed in school and remained determined. That spring, my mother met someone at the eating disorder clinic. She was the mother of an anorexic too, and as she told my mom her story, she made us realize our luck. This other girl did not stick it out. This other girl struggled so much that she ended up dropping out of school. She could not endure the pressures and judgments that existed within the dreaded high school walls. I was so close to following in the steps of that girl. I was so close to leaving school. I was so close to giving up. But I didn't, and for that I am proud.

Humiliation

Pure humiliation was all I felt as I stood there, broken and alone, sobbing desperately in the corner. My grandparents looked over at me. I felt the disgust and disappointment transfer from their eyes to my heart in one tense movement. At that point, I was almost positive that things between us could never be the same again. I was almost positive that they could never love me as much again.

Ten years earlier, I was their little princess. I'd spent the night at their house and snuggled with their stuffed animals. I helped make pancakes in the morning and cookies at night. When the rest of the family came over, I became the kitchen helper. When it was just the two of us, grandma took me shopping and bought me ice cream. On days when we felt extra adventurous, she'd take me into Washington, DC on the Metro and we'd explore the different museums. When the weather was nice, we went to the nearby park and she pushed me on the swings for hours. I was innocent. I was clueless. We all were. We were clueless of what the future would hold.

Now I was older. Now I was grown and my innocence had disappeared. My visits with my grandparents were less frequent and not nearly as intimate. I no longer found pleasure in museums and parks and ice cream. I wasn't their sweet, little granddaughter anymore. We knew what my life had become. The past was blissful, the future still unknown, but we all knew that night I was out-of-control.

I was screaming at the top of my lungs. It was a loud, shrill scream that echoed throughout our quaint house. Anger flashed across my face and I threw the plate on the floor. My dinner sprawled across the room as the plate hit the ground and shattered. I refused to eat. I couldn't eat. I wouldn't eat. My mom glared at me, trying to gain composure as she shielded off her annoyance. I felt lost, hopeless, and unable to stop myself. I tried to grasp my thoughts but there were too many. They swirled around my mind, making me unable to focus. The only thought I comprehended was my need to avoid food. I furiously banged my fists on the table. I was on a rampage and my mom began to fear what would happen. She was left alone to handle me, but she realized she needed help.

Picking up the phone with her shaking hand, she managed to dial the number. My grandma picked up on the other end and listened with worry as my mom begged for her help. Only seconds after hanging up the phone my grandparents piled into their car and began the drive. They arrived at my front porch in record time.

When I saw their car pull into the driveway I ran and hid. I sat crouched behind the bed like a little girl playing hide and seek with her friends. The only difference was that I sat there with tears streaming down my face. I could feel another scream making its way through me. It felt like I was going to vomit as I opened my mouth and let the scream tumble out. As the deafening sound hit the air, I could see a look of shock on my grandma's face. That was when it happened. That was my first experience of pure humiliation.

My grandparents made their way through our house. It was obvious that some sort of tornado had just occurred. There were papers sprawled everywhere and broken plates scattered over the floor. There was a hole in the wall and a broken door to the right. A tornado had definitely hit. That tornado was my eating disorder. The tornado took over and used me to destroy my surroundings. There was no denying it. My grandparents spotted me and the look on their face said it all. It was a mixture of confusion, disappointment, anger, and dread. They saw me for what I was: a mixed-up, destructive anorexic with no self-control.

A new plate was placed in front of me. My grandparents stand beside it, backing up my mom. I fully intended to eat it that time. No way was I letting them see me like this. I felt a need to straighten up, to redeem myself. But as I sat down, it took hold of me. It suffocated me and forced me to let out another sob. As soon as the sob was released, I felt the other emotions escape as well. Suddenly, it was happening again. I was screaming and crying and throwing and banging. This time there were more witnesses. This time three people sat and watched as I slowly went insane. I don't remember what happened next, my memories of the breakouts are a blur. However, I'll never forget the look on my grandma's face as she watched with shock.

Now I know that nothing will be the same. Each time I see her, I am reminded of that look. She told me she loved me. She told me she understood. My parents told me she understood. But I knew they were wrong, they were all wrong. No one understood, especially not my grandparents. This eating disorder had a stronger hold on me than anyone could ever imagine and there was more to it than met the eye. I knew that my actions were not my fault. I knew that I couldn't be held responsible when my eating disorder took control. But they did not. They did not know. They may have said they knew, but only I knew the truth from the way my grandma looked at me that day. I knew that I had forever changed in their eyes.

Eating in front of my grandparents remains my hugest struggle. Each meal I eat in their presence brings me angst. I feel as though I'm being watched, as though they're waiting for me to scream and cry. I feel ashamed knowing that they have seen me at my worst. I feel like scum when I remember that look. For me, I think it's impossible for it to ever be the same again. I know they can forgive but I also know that neither they, nor I, can forget. But at the same time, I know that there is still love. I know that each comment they make is fueled with good intentions. I know that with each breakdown I have, they will still love me, they will still accept. I just hope that one day I will make them proud. One day I hope I can look at them and know that I am not a disappointment.

Depression

Depression has become a word that is often used too lightly within our society. People use it to describe every little problem they have. If they miss a TV show it's "depressing." If they can't afford new shoes, they feel "depressed." It seems like people misuse the word to describe small mishaps. But real depression is more severe. Real depression is unbearable and serious. Real depression is deadly.

Those first six months of recovery, I was mired in layers and layers of depression. And I don't mean the temporary kind. The depression I felt seemed everlasting. It was a permanent dark cloud that settled right above my head. It was a tunnel of darkness that continued to suck me in deeper as the days passed. Eventually, it got to a point where I would rather die than live. Death suddenly seemed more appealing than life. Each day I felt more guilt, anguish, anxiety, fear, and anger. Each meal I struggled and hated myself. Each second, I thought more about suicide.

Recovery took us by storm. All of a sudden, there was no possibility of being carefree as every hour presented a new obstacle. The days were filled with fear. I feared the food. I feared gaining weight. I feared losing control and putting my trust in my parents' and doctor's hands. I feared letting go of my eating disorder.

Because the fear was so overpowering, it led me to do some undoubtedly desperate things. I quickly fell into extremely uncivilized routines. Before each meal I would run around the family room ten times in an attempt to get out all my anxious jitters. When the food was placed in front of me I'd begin to feel antsy. I felt emotion build up inside me. The only way to express these emotions seemed to be jumping up and down. In between the running and jumping, I would fill the air with piercing screams and desperate sobs. I knew how insane I was acting, but I also knew that I had no way of controlling it. My thoughts and actions were being dictated by the eating disorder. There was nothing I could do. I was completely possessed. At times, the food placed in front of me seemed so terrifying that even my usual displays of emotion were not enough. When I was having a particularly weak day or was faced with a particularly tough food, I'd take more drastic measures. I would throw myself on the ground, begging my parents to give me a break. I would dig my nails into my arm and try to squeeze out all my frustration. After doing so, I still felt angry, and I was left with scratch marks along my arm.

My depression spiraled out of control. The worst was when my depression combined with my eating disorder and caused me to go insane. Thoughts flooded my head, telling me that eating a certain food or giving in to a certain task would ultimately ruin my life. I was so convinced of this that I became determined to avoid whatever was thrown my way. I felt it was necessary to do whatever I could to remain skinny and in control. On bad days, I tried to run away. I tried to escape the decisions and worries. I tried to escape my world of pain. But my parents would always chase after me, or worse, threaten to call the police.

Unfortunately, my attempts didn't stop there. Every so often, the meal scared me so much that I could think of nothing more appealing than ending my life and committing suicide. At that moment, I had limited ways of doing so and the only idea that came to mind was choking myself. Obviously, that didn't turn out too well. I squeezed my neck and prayed that I'd soon be rid of all my fears and all my sufferings. Fortunately, my parents intervened and pleaded with me to calm down. Usually, it took hours before our house returned to more civilized peace. I'd end the disaster sobbing in my parents arms and crying "Why me? Why did this have to happen to me?" I'd beg for forgiveness and burst with regret. Each episode ended with something broken. Whether it was a plate, a door, the skin on my arm, or even just our souls, nothing withstood the day unharmed.

Needless to say, surviving each day was a struggle. Even when the meals were far off and the episodes were long gone my thoughts continued to revolve around suicide. Each minute of each day was a struggle and there was no escaping my obsessive thoughts on food and the guilt it brought me. It seemed unfair. I felt as though everyone else got a break in between meal times except for me! My family could take a few hours to compose themselves, but I still had to listen to the voices telling me I was fat, worthless, and stupid. I still had to listen to the vicious attacks of my eating disorder. I still had to listen to the mental calculating of calories and the brainstorming of ways to avoid food. Living life this way was torture. Living life this way was unbearable.

The depression and desperation I felt through these long, hard months went way beyond the disappointment of missing a TV show or not getting new shoes. The depression I felt was intense and shattering. It's a miracle I made it through. It's a miracle I forced myself to continue on.

Silver Linings

My life has pretty much been a dry, lifeless desert this past year of recovery. Nothing has sparkled or grown or brought light to my life in a while. Every day of recovery is tough to say the least. But to say that nothing positive emerged would be a stretch. Because actually, if I think about all the details long enough, I realize that the expression "every cloud has its silver lining" is a truer than I expected. The cloud over my life this past year was massive and gray; there wasn't much sunshine. Even still, the silver linings exist, reminding me that not everything in the world causes despair.

Maybe our family isn't exactly perfect. My brother is a pushover, my mom is a worrywart, my dad pushes himself to extremes, and I...well we all know what my problem is. But one thing in our household is for sure—we all love each other and would do anything to help one another succeed. This truth became even more evident in those long months of recovery. Probably the most positive benefit from this experience was how close my family became. For one, we started eating meals together every single night. Sure, the atmosphere of these meals wasn't exactly pleasant. Okay I admit it, they sucked. But at least we started seeing each other on a more regular basis. We also started family therapy, which brought on a lot of fighting, but also allowed us to get to know one another in a way we never had before. And then there's the fact that we had to go through a traumatic experience together. There's just something about sharing someone's pain that creates a close bond. I guess it stems from the need for support. When each person in our family needed support, we turned to each other. We were inseparably bonded by my eating disorder and the knowledge that we could get through it together.

So what if the eating disorder had caused difficult family fights? At least through it all, we stuck together and supported one another.

Then there's my dog—my silly, fluffy, stupid dog. We got Luc from a shelter when I was in fourth grade. He was the answer to my prayers. All my life I had wanted a dog and then finally, there he was, white and chubby and energetic. From the moment we met Luc we all fell in love. For the first few years I pampered him constantly and never wanted to leave his side. I walked him and brushed him and loved him. I taught him new tricks and showered him with attention. But over time, my adoration began to fade. It wasn't that I didn't love Luc anymore. No, he was my dog and I would always care. But as middle school began and my social life picked up, I didn't have as much time for him. I'm not sure when it happened but over time, the dog and I grew apart. I petted him only every so often and never walked him. My mom took over the duty of Luc full time. And it showed in his attitude. He followed my mom around as if they were attached at the hip and barely even looked twice at me.

It made me sad, but at the same time I had plenty of human friends; he just didn't seem all that important. But that was last year. That was before I realized that the love a dog gives was much stronger than love from friends. A dog's bond with his owner is unbreakable. They love you unconditionally. A dog doesn't realize when you make a mistake. As long as you fed, brushed, and walked your dog, all seemed good in the world—dog's heaven you might call it. In fact, the only reason Luc lost interest in me was because I had lost interest in him. But as soon as recovery started, that all began to change.

My new schedule required me to spend most of my days at home. My lack of a social life resulted in me spending nights lounging around the house, obsessing over food. I began to see a lot more of Luc, and he began to notice. He could sense my depression and he began to be my cuddle buddy. He snuggled up with me on the couch when I felt sad and once he waltzed over to look at me when I was crying violent tears. Most of my friends had deserted me, but even though I had neglected Luc for so long, he was still there, looking up at me with those cute brown eyes. Since then, I walk Luc all of the time. He obviously loves me for it; he's sitting by my feet as I am typing this. Knowing that he'll be there to wag his bouncy tail every morning always makes me feel a little better when times get tough.

Another silver lining was TV. Okay, bear with me, I know that sounds a lame. But you have to understand that my eating disorder hardly ever let me watch TV. Now I know that sounds insane. How could watching TV possibly have anything to do with an eating disorder? But believe me, the answer is a lot. Each time I sat down to watch a show, I immediately felt lazy and fat. The way my eating disorder saw it, time I spent watching TV could be put to better use doing something active like taking a walk. So I forbid TV. I just couldn't deal with that guilt on top of the constant guilt I felt from my new eating schedule. There was only one show that I could watch that made me fell nothing but content. It was the show Meredith and I had bent over backward for that past summer. It was the show that I owned DVDs of seasons 1, 2, and 3. *One Tree Hill* was my healthier addiction. I was obsessed with the quirky lines, intense scenes, heartwarming love stories, and incredibly gorgeous characters. And lucky for me, the new season was starting in January. I wished it had started earlier so that I could have watched it during those first recovery months, but at least it was back; I couldn't complain. Having the show on every Monday gave me something to look forward to each week. It became a family event. My parents and brother would sit down with me each new episode. To this day I'm still not sure if it was to watch the show or to see a smile on my face. But either way, it was always a rewarding night. It was the bridge connecting the old Nicole to the new one. It was the gateway that reminded me of everything normal.

Then there was the reward of my many small accomplishments. Pushing through the tough times didn't seem quite as bad when I had praise to look forward to when I made it through. Eating my first bowl of ice cream was hard, but at least I got showered with "good job" and "we're so proud of you" when it was all over. And there were so many bigger rewards to shoot for as well. For example, regaining the opportunity to play soccer or getting to choose my own breakfast.

Overall, most days sucked. And over all, life was pretty much a lifeless desert. But the silver linings were present, no matter how hidden. And when I think about it, that lifeless desert had some random patches of luscious green plants, reminding us all that maybe someday, it would all be okay.

Thanksgiving

My aunt's famous sweet potatoes sat on the table, covered in marshmallows and brown sugar. There was a basket of homemade, freshly baked dinner rolls to the right and a bowl of green beans to the left. There was a colorful salad, full of bright red peppers, purple radishes, leafy greens, and orange carrots. A mug filled with thick gravy sat on the edge of the table and a bowl of buttery mashed potatoes accompanied it. The turkey was carried in and carefully placed in the center of the table. Plates, wine glasses, and napkins were spread out along the white tablecloth, surrounding all the foods. In the next room, the grown-ups were laughing as they drank their wine and caught up with each other. Downstairs, laughter filled the air as the little kids scrambled around playing tag. Outside the window birds chirped and squirrels scurried around. The trees held leaves of every color, filling the sky with layers of gold, red, orange, and yellow. The cool, crisp November air blew across the porch as the sun began to set. It seemed like a typical Thanksgiving Day. It seemed as if the world was at peace. But then again, things aren't always what they seem.

When the family settled into their seats and bowed their heads to say a prayer, I was not with them. I was part of the family, yet I was not with them. Instead, I was downstairs. Instead, I was alone. I was in the guest room psychotically running in place and pushing myself to do hundreds of crunches. I snuck in exercise while trying to ignore the chattering and laughter coming from above. I tried not to think about the fun I was missing out on. I focused my thoughts on burning calories. I focused my thoughts on all the fatty foods I was avoiding and all the scary choices that I didn't have to make. Not sharing Thanksgiving dinner with my family was lonely, but my eating disorder had convinced me that it was the only way.

In October our plan for Thanksgiving was quite different. We were traveling to Colorado to spend the holiday with my mom's family. That was the plan and that was the way I wanted it. Colorado is my favorite place in the world. Without a doubt, I'm a mountain girl. Spending time with that side of my family always boosted me up. So I was more than happy to spend the holiday out there. But vacationing with my eating disorder was nearly impossible. As the day grew closer, we realized that I was not improving as rapidly as we had hoped. With only two weeks left until the trip, I still couldn't get through a meal without screaming, crying, or acting out; the eating disorder still had control over our lives. As time progressed so did my fear that my parents would cancel our trip. Finally, after many long, unbearable family discussions, the heart-shattering decision was made: we would postpone the trip.

At first the cancellation hit hard. I had looked forward to nothing but that trip over the last few months. I needed it. I needed to escape from my normal, everyday life. I needed a fresh atmosphere. I needed a change of pace. But, I knew that the decision we made was the right one. I was a mess both emotionally and physically, and there was no way I could improve that quickly. When it came down to it, I could not imagine how difficult it would be if my family in Colorado saw me like this. The trip was impossible and unnecessary. But the decision to stay home still hurt.

Even worse, I realized that we might not celebrate Thanksgiving at all. Traveling was impossible, but even here I didn't know how I would sit down at the table and participate in a feast in public. I had the same problem whether we were in Colorado or not. Thanksgiving would be difficult no matter which way we looked at it. We needed a plan. We needed a way out.

At first, I thought we should ignore the holiday altogether. My parents were willing to stay home and deal with me instead of getting together with our family at my grandma's house, and that plan sounded perfect to me. But as time went on, I realized how incredibly ridiculous and selfish that plan was. Just because I couldn't handle all of those foods didn't mean my parents should miss out too. Guilt rushed through me as I thought about how much my family had already sacrificed for me that year. I had taken over their lives like the Nazis took over Poland. I was dictating everyone's schedule and altering everyone's emotions. I couldn't deprive them of a quality family holiday as well. I just couldn't.

It was my brother who came up with the idea. He came up with a way to handle the holiday. He revealed the solution in family therapy. He reminded us that after a family feast, we usually took a family walk around my grandparent's neighborhood. He reminded us that if I chose to stay behind, I could have the house to myself. So that was it. My genius of a little brother quickly solved all our frets and questions. My cousins, aunts, uncles, grandparents, and parents would settle in for the meal as usual while I waited downstairs. Then when they were done they would leave for a walk, with the exception of my parents who would stay behind. Finally, our plan would end with my parents serving me my own, separate dinner that I would eat in private before the others returned. It was a plan, sure, but it most definitely was not a typical Thanksgiving.

Depending on how I choose to look at it, that day was a success. Everything happened the way we expected, and there were no mishaps along the way. But I ended the day with a void in my heart. I had spent the majority of the day by myself. I had spent the majority of the day with only my eating disorder for company. I had sat aside while my cousins played and my parents laughed. I was part of the family, only I wasn't. I was Nicole, only I wasn't. Nothing felt the way it should. Nothing felt right.

I took a step forward in an effort to erase the lonely feeling. I told my mom that I would join the family during dessert for pumpkin pie. I know this statement left my parents utterly shocked. It left me utterly shocked as well. However, they showered me with praise that I'm not sure I deserved. At the time, I convinced myself I was doing it to be included and to prove to everyone I was strong. And most likely, that was my main reason for taking the plunge. Yet there was another motive that I only now realize as I look back on that day. There was that know-it-all voice inside of me saying "if you eat pie they will be so proud that you could get away with eating very little of it." I knew I could clearly show my struggle to take even one bite and then use that struggle to my advantage. Don't get me wrong, that wasn't my motive. But I do believe that the thought of eating a minuscule amount of dessert instead of my usual was a major statement. And in the end, I was right. I ate just a sliver of the pumpkin pie, yet I still received pounds of gratitude and pride. And best of all, for a second I felt like part of the family again. For a second, it seemed like a typical Thanksgiving. But then again, things are not always what they seem.

Group

Some books on anorexia advise parents to avoid entering their anorexic into a group. The books caution that anorexia groups can be a way for the patients to band together in the wrong way. It can lead to a support group for anorexia instead of against it. However, I am truly blessed that my mom ignored these opinions. Entering group therapy was, without a doubt, the best decision my family and I have made during the process of recovery. Entering group changed my outlook. Entering group changed my life.

As I endured the torture of recovery, one feeling held strong above all else: the feeling of loneliness. I felt like I had no one because no one understood. I felt that my doctors and parents and friends knew nothing about me, nothing about this. I felt misunderstood. But then group came along, and suddenly, I wasn't alone. Suddenly, I could relate to others and share my thoughts without getting disapproving, confused stares in return. Suddenly, I had true companions.

My first group session was inspiring. There were just three of us, and one of the other girls was participating for her last time. Her departure from the group came for a positive reason. She no longer needed it. She no longer needed her eating disorder, and she no longer needed help. As I sat there, fresh out of the hospital with no clue of what was to come, I listened to her with hope. She was late to arrive because she had track practice earlier that afternoon. She was beaming with excitement as she told us about all the relays she had participated in and the upcoming island vacation she would be going on. Her life seemed perfect to me, who was suffering from the prohibition of sports and lack of excitement. When it was my turn to describe my week, the mood in the room changed completely. I released the memories of yelling matches and hospital threats. I released the pain of not being able to exercise and having each meal supervised. If her life was heaven, then mine was most definitely hell. But to my surprise, I caught her nodding her head as I babbled on. She surprised me even more with what she said next.

"I remember those days. That's exactly how my life was for a long time. It was torture not running track, and it seemed like all we ever did in the house was scream and cry. Supervised meals are the worst, but eventually, you'll get the control back. It just takes time."

As the words flew out of her mouth, I could tell how true they were. It was obvious this girl meant every part of it. She felt my pain from the past. She held my hopes for the future. She was living proof that the doctors were actually right when they told me "it won't be like this forever." One day, I will find happiness again. Now I knew it was possible. Now I had something to work for.

The next few months of group were not as helpful. There were only two of us in group, and the girl I shared with was at such a different place in her life that I could barely relate. She had never endured supervised meals and she currently had no obsessive thoughts about food. We were obviously two different people with two different fights against this disease. Each week, I would pray for someone to appear that I could relate to, that I could connect with. The girl was also getting ready to quit group and I knew it wasn't possible to continue on with just one person. I needed a new member to join. I needed company. I couldn't go back to feeling alone.

Finally as the other girl left, a new girl arrived. She was everything I had hoped for. She was everything I had been. She was everything I needed. Her name was Jane and she was in ninth grade, just like me. She had a younger brother in seventh grade, just like me. She had spent a week in the hospital, just like me. Only her diagnosis had come three months after mine, and three days before Thanksgiving. She had been diagnosed and put in the hospital immediately afterward. She knew what it was like to endure supervised meals and miss school for appointments. Jane was somebody who understood me. Jane was somebody I could trust. We immediately connected and her support helped drive me to make progress. But just as we grew closer, another girl was thrown into the mix.

This girl was confident, beautiful, and strong. Everything about her made her likeable from the start. She always had a smile on her face, and she was always throwing out positive reinforcements. Kate was a senior and she had been battling anorexia for about a year. She seemed so sure of herself and so brave against her disorder. She was everything I wanted to be. She was a role model and a shoulder to lean on. However, she did make her share of mistakes and needed our help in return. We were all there for one another. It was me, Jane, and Kate—the three friends who struggled together against anorexia. Going to group on Monday evenings became the only hour of the week that I enjoyed. It was the only hour of the week when I could laugh and open up. I could say anything I wanted without feeling stupid, because no matter how irrational the thought, the girls always understood where I was coming from.

It was different hearing things from them than it was from my parents or doctors. They weren't just speaking from what they researched or read in a book, they were speaking from their life experiences. Our hours together always sped by because we laughed and joked around until the clock shook us back into reality, telling us it was time to leave. But we refused to depart until the next session. No, we stayed connected. We had each other's cell numbers and Facebook profiles. When I was really struggling and needed help, I knew I could call either of them and find just that. They knew they could call me in return and they often did. Or even when I just wanted someone to complain to, they were there. I didn't even feel bad doing so because they almost always had similar complaints. We shared a bond that went deeper than any other. We shared a struggle, a fight, and a desire to win.

When I was first told that another girl would be added to the group I was unusually disappointed. The three of us were already so close and I didn't want another girl to come in and disrupt our happy group. What if she didn't understand us as well as we understood each other? What if she didn't fit in? I know it was mean, but I was content with group as it was; I didn't want it to change. The new girl was quiet. She didn't talk, and when she was asked a question she would give us no more than a one-word answer. She seemed uncomfortable around us, and it was a struggle to get her to open up. It seemed that my fears of adding a new girl were not unrealistic.

I don't know when she changed. I guess it was gradual, sneaking up on us without making a sound. Or maybe it was so sudden that it left us in a shock. I don't know how it happened, but one day I realized she was talking. One day she began to open up. Her thoughts and issues and questions poured out of her like a fountain. She was letting herself open up. She was blending in to our unit of support. She was becoming another member of our close-knit group. Her sudden confidence shone light on a whole new side of her. I realized how nice, funny, and understanding she was. I realized she too was someone I could trust.

As the months went on, more girls were added to the group. One girl had been going through recovery since she was twelve, which in total was six years! She made me feel blessed for how quickly I had confronted my problem. To me, it seemed as if recovery had been going on forever, but to her, it literally had. She had never experienced a normal teenage life, so she didn't feel as if she had anything to work toward. Then there was a girl who had been recovering for a year but was a year younger than Kate. Over time, new people joined and old people left. Each girl had her own battle, but each girl was familiar in every way. I saw myself in these girls. In some, I saw my past. In others, I saw my future. As a result, I found the present. I found friends and helpers and supporters. I found a connection that I never thought existed. Being part of group and knowing these amazing, beautiful, gifted girls taught me something I'll never forget—they taught me what it means to be understood. They taught me that my mind could deceive me. And most of all, they taught me that I'm not alone.

Therapy

Besides group therapy there are two other types of therapy I had been going to on a regular basis since my first week out of the hospital: individual therapy and family therapy. Each one helped me in different ways but I preferred individual therapy without question.

The day I met my individual therapist for the first time was just three days after my release from the hospital. She asked me if I thought I was anorexic. I guess that my answer took her by surprise, because when I replied, "I don't think…I know," her eyes widened and a smile crept on her face. She realized that counseling me would be easier because I'd already gotten past the denial stage. Her name was Lili. She was young, beautiful, and kind. She gave off a positive vibe that made me instantly like her. She listened intensely to all of my complaints and frustrations. That's what I needed. I needed someone to listen. I needed someone to listen but not judge. That's exactly what I found in Lili.

Our first few sessions were filled with my voice. She barely got a word in because she had a lot to learn about my life. I tried to reminisce on all the years I could vividly remember and worked at painting her a picture of my current life as well. I told her about all the relationships I had and how I felt about each person in my life. I told her what I had thought when I woke up that morning and what I was thinking as we spoke. I informed her on my theories as to why I got sucked into the eating disorder. I went on and on, and she continued to listen. Never once did she look bored. Never once did she roll her eyes at my mistakes or laugh at my fears. Even better, she seemed to actually understand. Every so often, when I was forced to stop and take a breath, Lili would add in a comment that would prove to me she cared. She would say simple things like "wow that seems hard" or "I can't believe you did that! That was really brave!" But as she spoke, her voice didn't sound even the least bit fake. Each word she spoke seemed to come from the heart. As a result, I began to feel less like a psycho. I began to feel less crazy. I began to feel like finally someone else could validate my fears and tell me they weren't ridiculous.

Lili also suggested techniques to regain my self-control. She tried to teach me soothing techniques such as deep breathing, but none I felt actually worked. It wasn't the techniques she taught me that helped. Instead, I feel I most benefited from finding someone understanding to talk to. Lili encouraged me to write and marveled at the brilliance of my flower arrangements. She pushed me to pursue the hobbies I loved the most and talked to me about topics such as music and movies. The thing I love the most about Lili is that when she talks to me I don't feel like she's doing it for her job or for money. When she talks to me I feel like she genuinely cares and has a desire to help. I know I can trust her, and at times she is the only one who knows my deepest secrets.

My dad often questioned whether seeing her was truly helping, but that summer I think he was proven wrong. That summer our schedules made it difficult to see each other. At times I would have to go three weeks without a Lili appointment. It was hard to manage those weeks because I didn't have anyone to vent to or to give me considerate advice. I fought more with my parents during those Lili-less weeks, and felt more depressed and alone. I know at times patients have to go through changes with their therapists, but I hope that I will always have a way to contact Lili and she will remain my therapist for as long as possible. Yeah, this year has been filled with bad luck. But when it comes to a therapist, I couldn't have gotten luckier.

Family therapy is a much different story. Our first family therapy session left us all in tears. It left me in hysterics actually. It was the weekend after the hospital. It was the session where we let him know about our lives and what had happened. Unlike with Lili, I didn't have time to explain myself and make him understand. Instead, my parents took up most of the talking time. And, to nobody's surprise, most of the talking revolved around me. That first session should have been titled the "let's complain about what Nicole's eating disorder has done to us" session. It seemed as though all my parents did was complain about me. They complained about the pain I caused them. They complained about the choices I had made. They complained about the person I'd become. Never had I felt as unloved and disconnected than I did during that hour. The next few appointments got a little better but they still left me bitter and lonely.

The purpose of family therapy was to bring our family together. However, I can't help but feel like it constantly kicked me apart from the rest. I always felt ganged up on. I always felt as though I was a disappointment. They always told me that I was doing something wrong. Instead of talking about our family issues, we talked about my eating disorder issues. And yeah, I get that my eating disorder is a big part of our family and that it needs to be talked about, but at the same time, it's not our only issue. There are other parts to our family that need to be talked about. There are other parts of us that we shouldn't ignore.

I may not like going to family therapy, but I could see that the therapist meant well. He was always giving suggestions, some helpful while others were not. He meant well, but I guess I just didn't like being the center of all our discussions with him. Sometimes I wished that my family would just give me a break.

Overall, therapy can help, but it can also be a huge pain. At the most suicidal points of my recovery, I found myself going to four therapy sessions a week! Group and family therapy were once a week and Lili was twice a week. At times, it got pretty overwhelming. I grew sick of expressing my feelings and sick of hearing advice. Most of all, it was hard to balance all the therapy with my schoolwork. I was still pressuring myself to get straight A's but barely had any time to study or finish my homework. Eventually, my parents and I decided to tell my teachers about the situation. It was the only way they'd give me a little slack and allow me more time to make up work that I missed.

So when second semester came around, I sat down and composed an email to send out to each of my teachers. I explained the difficult situation and informed them of the many therapy, nutrition, and doctor's appointments I had to attend week to week. I gave them a brief synopsis of the mental struggle and asked them to please be patient with me if I wasn't fully there or turned work in late. However, I did promise them that I would do my best to get everything in on time and that I would not take advantage of their relaxed attitudes toward me. Some teachers responded with their sympathies and some didn't respond at all. But each of my teachers followed through with their part as I followed through with mine. That whole semester I pushed myself to finish assignments whenever I got the chance. I barely ever turned something in late and when I did, it was only by a few days. But let me tell you, that was one stressful semester. The help therapy gave me was worth it, but the price I had to pay was steep.

Running Scared

It was the weekend after Thanksgiving, and my mom was taking me to the outlet mall to go shopping. We were planning to walk around Leesburg, Virginia, and stop for a snack before heading home later that afternoon to eat lunch. It was going to be our first shopping trip together since starting recovery. Needless to say, I was excited and eager to go. My mom had been telling me how much she missed our mother-daughter shopping over the past few months. And I understood. I missed those outings just as much. I too needed a break. I too wanted to have a little fun.

Recently, I've come to a realization about anticipation. Now I believe that if you set expectations too high, you are more likely to end up disappointed. My expectations for the shopping trip were about as high as it gets. I envisioned us bouncing around from store to store, laughing and talking, forgetting all our worries. But in reality, what occurred was completely the opposite, and I was left filled with regret.

When we arrived at the outlets around 9:00 a.m. that Saturday morning, dark clouds threatened the sky above us. We hurried into the first shop with hopes that the rain would hold off until noon. We browsed around, looking at shoes and handbags and jewelry, starting the day off to a positive start. But just fifteen minutes into our journey, a bang of thunder roared from the dreary skies. Slowly it began to rain. At first, it was light. I stepped out of the store and one solid, cold raindrop landed with a splat on the tip of my nose. As I took a step forward, several more drops pattered down onto my frail body. Goosebumps arose all over my arms and legs. Suddenly, it began to pour, making it clear that outlet shopping was no longer an option. But a ray of luck shone ahead of us as we remembered spotting an indoor mall about ten minutes down the road. We decided to hightail it over there and continue our shopping indoors.

It was just past ten o'clock when we arrived, and my snack time was approaching fast. Of course, knowing we would eat snack out that day, I had done my research. The night before, I had driven myself crazy, looking up calories of drinks at every coffee shop I could find.

Starbucks was the only place I had ordered from before and their hot chocolate proved to be my best bet. Surely this mall would have a Starbucks. There was nothing to worry about. So far, the day was running smoothly.

The second we walked into the mall, I noticed a bold, green sign. In thick lettering it read: "Starbucks—coming soon!"

Bam, right in the stomach. Someone had just punched me in the stomach. Or at least, that's what it felt like. This couldn't be true. Every mall has a Starbucks. Heck, it seems as if every street has a Starbucks! But as I frantically rushed to the mall directory, I was hit once again as I realized that this mall truly was Starbucks-free. Even worse, the one coffee shop open was Caribou Coffee. This was the worst it could've been. I had already investigated the number of calories in Caribou Coffee hot chocolate and they were way higher than my usual drink for snack. I just couldn't do it. I couldn't drink it. I'd be fat. I'd gain ten pounds. I'd be worthless. I couldn't. I wouldn't.

As my mom suggested we go there, I felt the eating disorder begin to take over. It slowly infested me with its venom, and began to control my thoughts and actions. There was no stopping it; it was already too powerful. I could feel the anger building up inside of me, and the urge to scream was beginning to develop. Already there were tears streaming down my face. It didn't matter that I was in public. In fact, I don't even think I noticed. All I could think of was avoiding that hot chocolate. I begged, yes begged, right in the middle of the mall, for my mom to find me another option. I pleaded, yes pleaded, for her to drive me to a place with a Starbucks. She tried to quiet me down, but her efforts were unsuccessful because of the annoyance and impatience that had developed in her voice. I could tell she was becoming frustrated and, in turn, I became frustrated. I knew I was losing control, but I had no idea how to stop. My sobs only grew louder as I realized how irresponsible I had become.

My mom stayed stern and refused to take me elsewhere. Trying to show that I could also hold my ground, I refused to eat. It was a power struggle, and I felt as though this was the only way I could win. But to my disgust, my mom simply replied, "If you don't eat then you'll just end up in the hospital again."

Fire, hate, death, bitch, black—words of anger fled through my head as I finally snapped. I felt trapped. I could not drink the hot chocolate after already making such a scene over it because that would be giving in. But I also could not end up in the hospital again, because I'd rather die than go through that torture again. My only option was to escape. I had to escape. I was angry and scared and depressed. I just needed to escape. That's all I could think about. I needed to get far away from those choices, from my problems. I needed to escape.

Before I knew what I was doing, I felt my feet begin to move. A burst of wind drifted past my face as people all around me sped by. I was running but I couldn't feel it. I was running but I felt unattached. It was as if I was watching myself from above; I was crying desperate tears as I weaved through the crowds of people. I couldn't stop. I heard my mom yelling after me and I saw the glares from the shoppers' faces, but I couldn't stop. Even if I had wanted to my feet would not slow down. I was running to the other end of the mall, but I felt as though I was running to the other end of my life. I was running away from my mom, but I felt as though I was running away from my problems. As I sprinted past the Caribou Coffee, a sense of freedom flooded through me. It was a sense of freedom that joined with the fear and regret and hopelessness. I was confused. I was overwhelmed.

I was such an emotional wreck, but suddenly, I began to laugh. Laugh! I was running away in the middle of an unfamiliar mall with tears in my eyes and an angry glare on my face, but I was laughing. It wasn't one of those happy laughs where the person thinks, "oh, this is funny" or "wow, this is fun." No, it was a sickening laugh. A laugh that emerged because that was all I had left. I was drained. I was cried out. I was angry. I was confused. I was so desperate that all I could do was stop there and laugh. My life had become so fucked up and I was sure there was no way I would ever be happy again.

I stopped to rest as I contemplated my options. I stared at the emergency exit on the opposite wall. I thought of running out and never returning. Then, I thought of what I would do after I ran out. Would I ask around for money so that I could buy myself a gun? And would the cashier even sell a gun to such a young girl? If I did get the gun, would I be strong enough to use it and daring enough to end my life? Or what if I just found an alley to sleep in for the night? Then maybe in the morning, I'd find a job at some restaurant or grocery store and start a new life. But could I manage without my parents, my brother, and my dog. What if I couldn't earn enough money for food and I starved to death? Or did I want to starve to death?

As I thought it over, I realized that these questions and choices were even harder than the questions and choices I already faced. Sure, I could run away and escape this life, these problems. But then wouldn't I face an even harder life and even more problems. I couldn't do it. I couldn't live, but I couldn't die. I was drained. I was desperate. I realized that all I needed right then was a hug. All I needed was for someone to take me in their arms, tell me they loved me, and assure me that everything would be all right.

I retraced my steps in an attempt to find my mom. But I did so with fear as I tried to prepare myself for her anger and scolding. After all, I had just run away from her, I had just gone insane. But, I needed her. I needed to go to her. I needed a hug.

When I saw her down the hall, I knew I was in for trouble. She looked angry, and she stormed up to me with fire in her eyes as she spotted me. I felt myself shiver with guilt and worry. I couldn't move. I was struck with the worst kind of depression. At that moment, I truly would have rather been dead. She yelled. She told me we were going home. She told me that I was never going to do that again. She didn't have to tell me I ruined our shopping trip—that much was already clear. The hate I felt for myself was overpowering. How could I have been so out of control? How could I have destroyed such a supposedly carefree day? She was mad. I was mad. But still, all I needed was that hug.

I mustered up a scrap of courage and asked her with a meek voice that reminded me of a child. I asked her for a hug. I stretched out my arms and prayed she would give me what I needed. She was mad. I was mad. But we both needed hugs. So that's what we got.

No Choice

"Just take her to McDonald's every day."
"Make her eat tons of milkshakes and cookies."
"She needs to start devouring juicy steaks and hamburgers."

Each onlooker had their own suggestions to give my parents. They all believed they had found a solution. They believed it was simple. As each person dished out advice, my parents nodded in agreement while secretly laughing at the naïve statements. Yet, they couldn't blame anyone for not understanding. I know for a fact that my parents were once just as naïve and clueless. They have admitted to thinking recovery would be easy and simple. It's because it's impossible to understand. No one can comprehend the true aspects of anorexia unless they live through it.

When the doctor first told us that recovery would be harder than anything we've ever endured, we all shrugged it off with ease. We heard what he was saying, but none of us could imagine how serious his warning truly was. As proof of our inexperience, my dad suggested to my mom that she serve me crêpes at an early point in my recovery. I had no idea what was coming. But from noticing the menu my mom reviewed the night before, I knew something unbearable was about to occur. I knew she was about to try something new, and let me tell you, I wasn't the least bit optimistic.

Then they made their first mistake. They called me down to the kitchen and delivered the plan. They told me they were ordering crêpes and I was allowed to pick three ingredients I wanted in mine. Now, to understand the error of this proposal, you must remember how unstable and possessed I was at that stage. I was just beginning the terrors of recovery, and my anorexia was stronger than ever. The second they gave me a choice I was overwhelmed with fear. There were so many options, so many combinations. Automatically, I started running them through my eating disorder and analyzing the possible fat and calorie content in each item. But everything I determined was just a guess because, obviously, the nutrition facts were not provided. I kept second-guessing myself, and my eating disorder began to go into overdrive. It was like a one-way tunnel. It couldn't see a straightforward right choice and a wrong choice. Each food had its flaws, which made finding the "right" choice nearly impossible. The thoughts spun through my head like a blizzard. I found myself gasping for breath. The room seemed to close in around me. I couldn't take it. I couldn't deal with the stress and the decision-making and the food. I started screaming and crying before my parents even ordered the food. After an hour of going back and forth in between my freak-outs, I settled on cheese and spinach. But the moment I stated my choice, guilt flooded through me, engulfing me. My parents ordered the food, but it would take time to prepare. That meant time for me to worry. That meant time for my eating disorder to push me around. That meant time for fear to build up.

Eating the crêpe was more difficult than any food I had been forced to eat before. It was huge and greasy. The cheese melted and oozed out of the crêpe. I tried to pick off a glob of cheese, but I couldn't because pinching it only caused it to stretch out for miles. It was my worst nightmare. By the time the food arrived I had already made a promise to myself not to eat it. My eating disorder had already convinced me that breaking this promise would ruin my life. And that's not an exaggeration. In the heat of the moment, with the manipulation of the anorexia, I completely believed that eating the crêpe would ruin my life. I was willing to do anything to stop this from happening. I had to prove I had the control. I had to prove I could resist the temptations and pressures.

The next few hours were packed with shrieking, pounding, throwing, crying, scratching, and anger. By the time I finished the crêpe, you could see the exhaustion on everyone's face, including my own. We were worn thin and drained. But I soon found, it wasn't over yet.

They made mistake number two. They ordered me to finish off the meal with a dessert crêpe. It would be the first time I had to eat a dessert, but definitely not the last. It was my first time eating chocolate sauce and whipped cream and it was all happening at once. I was already broken and depressed from the first course, but apparently that wasn't enough. I didn't think I even had any more tears or screams left, but as soon as the dessert landed on the placemat in front of me, I learned that I was wrong. I screamed and cried for another hour as I struggled to swallow the terrifyingly sweet crêpe. Needless to say, after the horrors of the meal that seemed as though it would never end, my parents decided never to feed me crêpes again. They were realizing that making me gain weight was not going to be as easy as they had hoped.

All the people who suggest fatty foods as a cure are under the same misconception that my parents were at one time. They believe that gaining weight just requires an increase in fattening foods. They believe that recovering from anorexia just means gaining weight. What they don't realize about the disease is the mental side that turns the simple task of gaining weight into months of extreme difficulties.

Gaining weight is only one aspect of recovery. It's only the physical half. The other half is mental and is way more complex. To recover mentally requires the patient to completely change their way of thinking and their outlook on life. It requires the patient to erase a whole section of their brain. It requires the patient to ignore the screaming voices inside their head. It requires the patient to face their worst fears. And doing all this is not a simple task. Doing this could take months or even years. Doing this takes strength, bravery and confidence.

Although all of the traits needed for recovery are hard to acquire, strength is, in my opinion, the easiest. Strength grows with each meal consumed and each internal anorexic command ignored. Strength comes hand in hand with time. As time progresses, so does the willpower. Finishing a difficult food or withstanding an intimidating meal builds your strength and knowledge that you can succeed. Each rebellion against the eating disorder makes it weaker. But strength doesn't come without suffering. To get strength, you need to get through meals. And to get through meals requires bravery.

Bravery is a bit more complex. Bravery doesn't just happen over time. You have to find bravery from within. For an anorexic, facing food is like being attacked by a shark or strangled by a snake. Many people fear vicious animals, reptiles, and insects; anorexics fear food, gaining weight, and losing control. If someone who is afraid of spiders is asked to hold a tarantula, they cannot easily oblige. They need to muster up bravery. Sometimes they cannot find the bravery the first time they are asked. Sometimes it takes multiple tries before they finally have the courage to complete the task. They may need to practice with smaller spiders first before they can make their way up to the giant tarantula. It's the same way with anorexics and food. There are some foods that I cannot, no matter how hard I try, face the first time they are placed in front of me. Sometimes it takes many attempts before I can finally eat the food or drink the drink. It took months before I had the bravery to eat foods such as ice cream, burritos, and chocolate. Before I could conquer those foods, I had to practice on others that were scary, but not as scary. And then there are foods that are even scarier. I have yet to find the bravery and power to eat pizza, french fries, or cake. But eventually I will. I just need to endure the hardships of my other fears and continue the pains of practice.

Confidence is the hardest trait to obtain. For me, and for most anorexics, confidence is non-existent. Part of what caused me to fall into the trap of my eating disorder was my incredibly low self-esteem. The way I viewed myself was about as crappy as it got. Each time someone gave me a compliment, a voice inside assured me they were lying. Each time I did something right, a voice inside told me what I had done wrong. Each time I found a plus, a voice inside pointed out a flaw. Resisting food and losing weight were the only ways I knew how to feel proud of myself. But during recovery, we were asked to do just the opposite. I was supposed to find the confidence to say YES to food and to GAIN weight. I was supposed to feel proud as I did while realizing the progress it symbolized. But how could I do that when I saw nothing good inside of me. When I looked at myself I saw failure and imperfections and mistakes. When I looked at myself I saw nothing but negatives. And when I ate, the negatives only grew stronger. When I ate, I only felt worse. For that reason, confidence was the most difficult to conquer. Finding confidence can take years of work. Finding confidence turned a simple task of gaining weight into a complex battle with a controlling disorder.

"Get Better." People constantly throw that phrase at me when they discover my eating disorder. They mean it to be comforting and sympathetic. But it frustrates and annoys me. They tell me to get better as if it were that simple. They tell me to get better as if it's really my choice. They know nothing. Can an alcoholic just "get better" because they decide to stop drinking? Can a drug addict just stop doing drugs with ease? Can anyone just erase their problems because they feel like it? No, of course they can't. And neither can I. No matter how badly I want to "get better" or how much I yearn for the issue to be in my past, I can't just make it happen. I can't just decide to stop being anorexic. That's what people don't understand. That's why I'm misunderstood. Anorexia is not a way of life. Anorexia is a sickness. Anorexia is not a choice. Anorexia is a disease.

Flirtation

I stood at the end of the street. My back was hunched over and tears were dripping from my face onto the cool asphalt below. My hair tangled as I desperately tried to bat it away from my face. I looked back toward my house to make sure no one was watching. I focused my eyes on the leaf that blew across the street as I poked my shaky hand down my throat. Wind swirled around me as I gagged and coughed. It was my first attempt at throwing up. It was a desperate plea to take back what I had just done. It was an unusual solution for me, but then again, it was an unusual time. To explain how I got there, on the side of the street shamelessly attempting to throw up the food in my stomach, let me go back to September. Let me go back to when the lie first began.

I was out of the hospital and struggling to begin the process of recovery. I was returning to school with no desire to make friends or to stay involved. I was returning to school with only one mission—to hold on to my eating disorder as tightly as possible. Doing so would provide me with the comfort of something familiar. I was just starting high school and had been absent for most of the crucial first weeks. I didn't know my way around and I didn't know a majority of the people around me. Everything was different. Different teachers and different classes were combined with the different location and different classmates. My life as a high school student was uncertain. There was only one aspect of life I knew, one aspect of life I could count on. Following the commands of my eating disorder felt safe and promising. It was what I was used to. It was soothing in a world of discomfort. For this reason, I was compelled to go against the doctor's orders to gain weight. I was compelled to ignore my parent's pleas to stop starving. I was compelled to disregard the need to let go of my anorexia.

I was told to have a snack during my fourth period when the other students were eating their lunch. Then I was supposed to come home and eat my own lunch after school with my mom. The weapons I was ordered to eat were an apple and a peanut butter bar. They foolishly trusted me to eat this alone. They expected me to eat this when there wasn't even anyone around to make me. But it was so easy. It was so easy to just throw it away. They had no proof of me doing so; therefore, I could easily get away with it. Each day I'd arrive to school and toss my lunch in the trash can within the first five minutes. Some onlookers would give me a leery look as they witnessed an unhealthy-looking girl dispose of a non-eaten lunch at 7:30 a.m. in the morning. But I didn't care. I didn't care what they thought of me. All that mattered was the surge of power that ignited me as I did this devious act. When I went home and was forced to eat lunch, it wouldn't feel quite as bad knowing I had avoided that one little snack.

Over time, however, my mom caught on to the immense opportunity she had been giving me. She asked me with doubt if I had really eaten my snack all those times. The moment she asked, I could feel my anger exploding. *How dare she doubt me! How dare she not trust me! I'm her daughter but she can't even believe me about this one, little thing!* I was appalled. It didn't matter that she was right. It didn't matter that I was lying. It didn't matter that I didn't deserve her trust. None of that seemed to make a difference. In fact, I don't think I even realized these things. I don't think I realized how deceptive I was being. All I knew was that she didn't trust me, and that made me furious. I needed her to know that I did what she told me to do—even though I didn't.

"I can't believe you'd even say that! Of course I eat it. Look, if you really can't trust me then I'll do something to prove it to you. Would it make you feel better if I saved my apple core to bring home and show you?" Before the suggestion even escaped my mouth, I already knew what I'd do to pull it off. The tricks and the lies—they all came so naturally. I didn't think twice about doing any of it. In my mind, I was just doing what was right and what everyone else wanted was always wrong. Not only was I deceiving those around me, I was deceiving myself.

That agreement was the beginning of a new routine. As I entered school that afternoon after returning from a doctor's appointment, I snuck into the basement bathroom and locked myself in a stall. Shamelessly I began biting into the apple. I quickly spit each bite out into my paper bag. I continued doing this until spit hang from my lips and a seemingly devoured apple rested in my hands. I made it look like I had eaten without having to swallow a bite. It was a cruel and conniving gesture. But oddly all I felt was pride. My eating disorder started feeding me compliments. It told me I was a genius for coming up with such a clever solution. It told me I was strong for disobeying my parents' and the doctor's commands. It told me I was powerful for making the choice about snack on my own. I was pathetic. I hovered over the trash with a bag of soggy, chewed-up apple pieces in one hand and a brown core of an apple in the other. And this became the routine of the next few months. It was a moment when I should have felt nothing but embarrassment; instead, I felt nothing but pride.

For a while, I managed to continue on like this, somehow avoiding the snacks on the weekends. Don't ask me how I did this because I don't remember. Some of the lies I told and tricks I played came so unconsciously that I don't even remember what I said or how I did it. All I know is that I made it all the way until the beginning of November without eating my snack. But it couldn't go on like that forever. Eventually it would catch up to me. And on that day, on the day I stood at the corner of my street, forcing myself to throw up, it finally had.

It was a complete shock. My mom called me upstairs around 10:00 a.m. in the morning and placed it in front of me. It was a green apple and a peanut butter bar. She was asking me to eat them. She was asking me to eat all of it right there in front of her. Immediately, the anxiety kicked in. I began to cry and shriek on my knees, begging her to change her mind. And I was caught.

"This is what you have been supposedly eating every day at school. If you were really eating it like you say you are then eating it now shouldn't be this hard."

One sentence, one sentence tore my world apart. I couldn't keep deceiving her. I couldn't keep lying. I had no way to hide it. And worst of all, I had no way to avoid the food. I felt like a surfer, lost in the middle of an ocean with a shark circling and no way to escape. My life was the ocean. I was lost in my life, my problems, and my fears. The food was like the shark, circling me and ready to attack. I feared that food like most people fear for their lives. I hated my mom. That's all I could think of. I hated my mom for doing this to me. Because that's how I felt. In that moment I was certain that this was my mom's fault. After all, she was the one forcing me to eat. I hated her. I had to stop her. I had to stop this from happening. Eating that food would be the last thing I'd do. It would be my last resort. I had to try any way possible to avoid it.

Before I knew what I was doing, I lunged at my mom. She held the food in her hand with a smug look on her face, obviously proud she had caught me in such a massive lie. I needed to knock the food out of her hand. I would destroy the food. I threw it at the ground and stomped on it and yelled at it. I screamed angry threats as I chucked the apple at the wall and ripped apart the bar's wrapper. I was so out of control that my mom needed to call a neighbor for reinforcement. And despite my attempts, the food was still placed in front of me since my mom had a closet full of peanut butter bars and a fridge full of apples. There was no escaping it. I had to give in. So I ate. I ate and I cried and I thought of death. I forced it down and felt heavy with guilt and anger. The moment I swallowed my last bite, the regret settled in and I felt insane. I ran out the door. I ran around the cul-de-sac. I ran sobbing to the corner of the street. That's how I got there. That's how I became desperate enough to try and make myself throw up. But fortunately, as hard as I tried, all I could do was gag. It seemed to me that I was such a failure I couldn't even throw up right. I reentered the house with self-pity and self-hate.

After the disasters of that Saturday, nothing was the same. I started returning home during my lunch period to eat snack with my mom. But I only had to return for fifteen minutes. I was to go back to my friends for the remainder of the period after finishing my job and taking my medicine, otherwise known as food. But returning to my friends was not an option. I didn't care about hanging around teenage girls and pretending like I wasn't secretly falling apart. I didn't feel like walking in late and being pounded with questions as to why I didn't arrive on time. I didn't feel like sitting in a cafeteria surrounded by girls who picked at their food. No, returning to my friends was not an option. Instead, I preferred to be alone.

The attempt to throw up was a moment of weakness. When I calmed down, I realized how foolish I was to try. I strayed away from the idea for about two months. I was becoming more successful in my recovery and no longer felt the same excessive level of desperation that I had on that crisp, autumn day. But as the desperation decreased, my weight increased. By the middle of December, the doctor's told me that my weight was heading in the right direction and they showered me with praise. Immediately after hearing the praise, my eating disorder joined in. Only my eating disorder was not giving praise, it was giving disapproval. It told me that if my parents were happy, then I was doing something wrong. It told me that my parents just wanted for me to be fat, and if I wanted to be skinny my parents had to be disappointed in me. The thought was twisted, I know. But at the same time, it seemed so logical. Hearing that things were going well somehow gave me a desire for things to go badly.

For one week in the middle of December I returned to my old desperate ways. For one week, I entered school after eating snack, locked myself in a stall, and spent up to ten minutes trying to regurgitate the just-consumed food. Each day I cried and felt shame. Each time, I hoped that throwing up would help me redeem myself, but each time, it just made me feel worse. On that last day, I stepped into the hall with my hair a mess, my eyes were puffy and red and still spilling tears. As I turned the corner, I was caught. Two of my friends were standing there. They were standing there and staring. A look of confusion swept over their faces. They were concerned over my tears. There was no way they could've known what I had just done; yet, somehow I felt guilty. I felt like they had discovered me. I felt like they had seen me for the pathetic disaster I had become. And in return, that's how I finally saw myself.

Hair

I was sick of being the person I had become. I was sick of looking in the mirror only to see the same face staring back at me each time. I was sick of letting my past define me. I was sick of all the baggage this past year had left me to carry. I was sick of being dubbed "the anorexic girl." I was sick of life.

But I had the perfect solution. It was pure genius. It was the cheapest way to disguise myself, the safest way to reinvent myself, and the quickest way to become more satisfied. All I needed was a fresh start. A new beginning to erase the past. The solution was quite simple really. I would dye my hair. It would be more efficient than going through the pain and hassle of plastic surgery. Besides, I didn't want to completely rearrange who I was. I just needed a boost to kick off my future. I just needed a change of hair color. That would certainly help me find the joy I had been missing in life.

My mom wanted me to go blond. I started out with dirty blond hair that darkened with every year. She told me I already had gorgeous hair. She told me the idea was absurd. However, she had to give me her opinion.

"If you do go through with this then you should stick to just a slight change. Lighten things up a bit with a blond highlight here or there. That should do the trick." Although she sounded sure as she spoke, I wasn't so convinced. I knew what I needed and a slight change was not it. I needed to make a statement. I needed to transform myself. And most of all, I needed to go dark.

Dark had become the definition of my life. The year was filled with dark discovery after dark discovery. Each time I found a gleam of light shining down on me, the hope was overshadowed by more dark despair. Nothing seemed to be going right, and everything seemed to be going wrong. My outlook on situations began turning dark along with my life. I thought of death multiple times during the day and began listening to sadder, slower music. Dark was me. And it needed to become my hair.

After weeks and weeks of begging and pleading, I finally convinced my parents to pay for the hair experiment. There was only one condition: I wasn't allowed to dye it myself; I had to have it professionally done. "No way am I letting you ruin that pretty hair of yours," my mother said. She shook her head and laughed as she turned back to immerse herself in a book once again. She thought I was being silly. But I knew she had it wrong. I wanted this so I could move on. I wanted this so I could mature.

Deep down, another benefit urged me to walk into the salon that early Saturday morning. It was the hope that my hair would be a distraction. Maybe it could be a distraction from my body, my weight, my look. Maybe it could even be a distraction from the rumors, the lies, the talking behind my back.

So as the sun rose and we yawned our way into the car and drove through the vacant streets to the quaint salon downtown, I had a plan. Nothing less than what I envisioned would be acceptable. I told the stylist what I wanted and sat back waiting to be awed.

The highlighting began. As we waited my mom continuously paced back and forth, throwing in comments wherever she could about how she hoped it wouldn't look too different. I groaned as she worried. It was clear we wanted different outcomes. But it was my hair, and I thought for sure the color would go my way.

Three hours later, the towel was ripped off. My new hair was unveiled and all around me were smiling faces. But as I looked in the mirror, a frown fought its way onto my face. As the people around me gasped I thought they were either complete idiots or blind. There was barely anything different about the face that darted its disappointed eyes back at me. I saw a chunk of slightly darker hair every so often but overall, nothing. It was still me. But I couldn't insult the hairdresser, but I could express my opinion. If I told her nicely, she might even fix it for me. I began to open my mouth but she beat me to it.

"Oh darling, look at you! I think this is the best look for you. I kept it simple to satisfy your mom, but honey, it's the perfect amount of change your hair needed. I'm so glad you like it."

What could I say? I could never tell her I hated it now. Her face would fall. She'd grow silent with shame.

It didn't matter either way. I couldn't tell her the truth; I knew that much for sure. So I smiled and said my most sincere "thank you" as I hurried out the door. But my fake attempts at happiness didn't fool my mother. She knew right away that something was up and once I expressed my true feelings the emotions began to slowly drip out of me like a leaky roof on a rainy day. Before I knew it I was crying. Oh, how I so wanted everything to go as planned. I put the vision on a pedestal. Again, my mistake was looking too forward to something, which set me up for disappointment.

Screw that, I thought, *my hair will become what I wanted no matter what*. And so it did. My mom dialed the number and made the appointment. The next morning we repeated the actions of yesterday's disaster only that time, we ended with a happier outcome.

Obviously this hair was crucial to me. My mom could see that her desires would not be met. She gave in and declared that all she wanted was for me to be satisfied with the end result. So we went at it again, this time making it clear that I needed a huge change. Nothing similar to what my hair had looked like before. Because wasn't that my goal with recovery? In the end we all wanted for me to be a better person. We wanted for me to be free of the eating disorder, free from the old me. At the end of recovery the change in my lifestyle would be huge. That was why I needed my hair to be different.

The face smiled. The eyes sparkled and gleamed with bliss as they stared at the reflection. This time, it wasn't anyone's face but my own. And this time, I felt happier, better, possibly even prettier. That was it. that was the beginning of the new me.

Christmas

The mistletoe hung from the trees. Snow began to fill the air and pile up on the streets. Joyful carols were sung and played everywhere I went. Colorful strings of light decorated practically every house. Christmas was here. It had arrived and so had we. Finally, we were in Colorado. It had been almost a year since we had seen everyone, the longest we'd ever gone. After the decision not to travel for Thanksgiving, the fact that we could manage it one month later seemed like a blessing.

I was happier than I had been in a while. I was always happier in Colorado. The landscape makes me smile. I'm a mountain girl at heart, there's no doubt about it. I'd take the views from the top of a steep mountain over the view from a tropical beach any day. But the setting isn't the only aspect of Colorado that I love. My family out there also lifts up my mood. Everyone there is loud, funny, and carefree. We can spend hours laughing with each other and it feels like everything in the world is right. Even the atmosphere is more positive. The Sunderland's, my mom's side of the family, are so laid back. This makes life seem less stressful because they're never in a rush or pushing to make plans. With them everything just happens when it happens, which is relaxing. I desperately needed that calm and peaceful environment. With all the crap that had happened to me in the last five months, I really needed a chance to relax and experience happiness again. I had high hopes for the trip and counted down the days until it arrived.

In the back of our minds, my family knew this trip wouldn't be the same as the previous trips. Although my eating disorder was improving, it was still a devil to live with. I still busted out screaming during meals and grew fidgety when eating in front of others. I still tried to get out of finishing things and occasionally threw a fit when my parents were strict with me. Our home life was not ideal. Going on a trip at this time would be difficult, but we had given it deep consideration and decided that, yes, it was manageable.

Our first problem arose when we were still at the Washington, DC airport, waiting for our flight. It was my snack time and my mom and I began to argue over which brand of chocolate milk I would drink. For weeks we had talked about how difficult following my meal plan would be on vacation. Because of that, I guess I just assumed I could get away with eating less. But it was evident that my mom did not have that in mind. She kept pushing me to drink all of the milk and finally threatened me by saying we wouldn't even go. We were so close to leaving and I knew I couldn't ruin it. I finally gave in but was in a bad mood the rest of the day.

When we arrived to my aunt and uncle's house later that day, my cousins, and grandpa were there too, waiting to greet us with smiles and hugs. For the first hour, everything was the way it should be. I was ecstatic to be there and, momentarily, I forgot I was anorexic. But the second my family mentioned dinner, the trip turned downhill. My parents and I had already decided that eating with my extended family was out of the question. I knew I couldn't keep my cool during meals, and I didn't want my extended family to see me at my worst. I couldn't deal with the embarrassment. Instead, we devised a plan for how I would eat separately. There was a huge basement that stored four dinner trays in the corner. The arrangement was that when meals came around, my parents would bring our food down while I set up the trays. We'd close the door and have privacy as I struggled to maintain order. It seemed simple but it was anything but. I quickly learned that quieting my eating disorder was not going to be as easy as I had hoped. Multiple times I found myself sprawled on the floor, screaming into a pillow. My parents spent hours trying to hush my sobs and bring me back to sanity. I couldn't help myself. I had thought that being around people who loved me would make my eating disorder go away. But that was not the case.

The worst episode happened one early afternoon at the nearby Subway. With hopes that I was strong enough, my parents took me there for lunch in the middle of the week. We had done it before, no problem. I ate a sub and a yogurt. At times, if I was brave enough, I'd even replace the yogurt with Baked Lays potato chips. But on that day, the issue arose around the drink. I was used to having eight ounces of juice or lemonade but the cups that came with the meals there were twenty ounces. My parents persisted that I drink it all because they claimed the rest of my meal was on the light side. But it didn't seem fair. There was more than twice the amount of lemonade in the cup than I normally drank.

Immediately, I let my eating disorder take over. I drowned in thoughts of how fat they wanted me to become and how unjust their commands were. I couldn't let them get away with it. I couldn't drink it all. But they wouldn't give up. Eventually, I became so angry that I ran out of the store. My parents were growing impatient and embarrassed. They forgot how hard meals were for me because they were stressed about trying to look normal in public. I was ruining their vacation and I could tell they were growing bitter. I refused to go back inside so my dad rushed over and yanked me forward by the arm. I started to scream, "Let go! Let go!" But this made him angrier. All of a sudden, he swung a punch at me, his fist ended two inches away from my face. He had no intention of actually hitting me; he was just trying to get his anger out, something I had struggled with numerous times. But his act startled me and I began to sob. They fought with me until I got in the car, barely able to catch my breath.

I was completely under the control of my eating disorder. I had lost myself to the disease and began kicking the driver's seat in front of me. My parents began to yell at me frustrated and desperate to get me to stop. This only made me more upset, causing my suicidal thoughts to reappear. I later found out that I wasn't the only family member to have thoughts of death that day.

The second we arrived back at the house, I ran upstairs and slammed the door. I crouched in the corner of the spare bedroom and began to cry. I needed to talk to someone who understood me. I needed someone who could sympathize with me. I whipped out my phone and dialed the first number that came to mind. I called Kate from my group therapy. She always had positive advice, and I felt as though we had really connected since we met. I knew that if anyone could help me, it was she.

I talked with Kate for close to an hour. Calling her was every bit as helpful as I had hoped. She let me vent and told me that she completely knew how I felt. She made me feel less alone by sharing similar stories of disasters that had happened to her in the past. It was nice to know I wasn't the only one who grew crazy around meals. It was nice to know that someone understood what I was going through and the mental abuse that came along with it. Best of all, she made me feel better about myself by telling me how beautiful and skinny she thought I was. I'd been told these things before, but only from my parents or other grown-ups. Somehow, hearing I was skinny from another anorexic sounded more believable. It made me feel positive to know that she viewed me that way.

Best of all, Kate assured me that I most likely had a super-high metabolism. The way she told me these things made me feel more at ease. She seemed so sure that I'd always be skinny. No matter how much I had doubted my future before, in that moment I believed it would all be all right. I thanked her from the depths of my heart as I wiped away my tears and hung up the phone. I was still full of guilt, regret, sadness, and anger, but I was determined to turn this vacation around. My parents had been downstairs booking us an early flight home. I knew I couldn't let that happen. I needed another chance to show everyone I was strong. I did everything I could and finally convinced my parents to stay. After that, the trip got a little better, but overall, it was still a huge letdown.

I guess the hardest part of that trip was the fact that I felt so disconnected from my family. We ordered pizza from our favorite place, as we did every visit. But I didn't eat it with them. I wasn't able to eat the pizza at all. Pizza still remained my scariest food and nothing would get me to face it, not even my loving, supportive family. Another day, my uncle brought home McDonald's for all the cousins. Yet again, I couldn't eat it with them. Yet again, I was left out.

But the worst part was on Christmas day. Sitting at a table with all those delicious homemade foods was something I could not find enough strength to do. I knew I would end up regretting it, but I was positive in my decision to not eat the Christmas meal with the rest of the family. Instead, I continued my routine of eating separately in the basement. As I lay on the couch alone, listening to the laughter on the floor above me, I felt a tear slip down my cheek. I felt so alone. I felt so disconnected. I felt so stupid and weak. I knew that it was my decision. I knew that, if I wanted to, I could waltz upstairs, plop down at the table, and dig in with the rest of them. But, even though I wanted this, I just couldn't. Even after five months of recovery, I hadn't figured out how to stop my eating disorder from controlling my life. Even after five months of recovery I was still holding on tight to the anorexia. Even after five months of recovery, my journey was not even a quarter of the way finished.

In that moment, I made a promise to myself. No matter what, next Christmas would be better. Next Christmas, I would be better. Next Christmas, life would be better.

Perfect

Perfect. The word is so complex, yet so simple. It means everything, yet it means nothing. It holds powerful control, yet it's uncontrollable. I strive for perfection, yet I cannot reach it. Perfect is a deadly word.

First semester of my freshman year was coming to an end, and perfection was constantly on my mind. Midterms were coming up. It was imperative that I succeed in every extent of the word. I had struggled during the first quarter due to the week of school I missed while being in the hospital, as well as the numerous classes I missed for doctor's appointments. Not to mention the jam-packed therapy and food schedules that took away valuable homework and study time. For those reasons, I ended the quarter with three B's and four A's. Miraculously, I obtained straight A's for the second quarter. Although I focused on those quarter grades, I realized they didn't matter. The only grades submitted to colleges were the semester grades, an average of the two quarters plus the exam grade. If I wanted to start off with straight A's when I applied for college, the exams would be my ticket. Getting a B was not an option. There was no other choice but to push myself to the limit. I had to come out on top. Most of all, I had to be perfect.

Review week for those first exams was hell. For any high school student, and especially freshmen, exam week was stressful to say the least. But I wasn't just any high school student. I encountered the usual stresses of studying, preparing, and worrying, as well as the stress from continuing my battle against anorexia and trying to gain weight. Each day held struggles with food, intense studying, screaming battles provoked by my disease, and more hard-core reviewing. That's all I did: sleep, eat, study, cry, eat, study, scream, cry, eat, and sleep again. To say I felt overwhelmed would be an understatement. My perfectionism teamed up with my anorexia to beat me to the ground. I was worn thin. Some may call it an emotional wreck, but I chose to call it chaotic determination.

The exams that worried me the most were in science and math. I needed A's on both to receive an A for the semester. They had always been my least favorite subjects and studying for them would not be easy. I felt the need for an extra boost. I wanted a tutor.

hen I told my mom, she wasn't convinced. She insisted that I was student and I always did well on big tests. If I applied myself I would reach my goal alone. But, she saw how important the tutor idea was to me and agreed to set up one appointment for the weekend prior to exams. In preparation, I reviewed all of my notes from the two classes so that I was prepared with questions when I met with the tutor. I did so with anticipation, hoping that the tutor would be helpful.

I was not let down. The tutor welcomed me with open arms and went above and beyond to make me feel confident. We tackled all of my weak spots and even reviewed some of my strong spots along the way. Yet, somehow I still felt uneasy. I went home and immersed myself in the depths of my notes one last time. The night before my first exam was full of intensity. That desire to be perfect burned inside of me. I yearned for the power to say that I had accomplished my goal, the power to say I was worth something.

It's hard to explain why getting a perfect report card was so necessary to me. I guess there were a lot of reasons. Most of all, it was because perfection was a feeling that had become nonexistent in my life. Ever since my diagnosis, I had felt more and more like a screw-up with each passing day. That feeling of worthiness I had once felt when turning down food was gone. The feeling of pride from losing weight was hidden under a pile of guilt. Nothing in my life was under my control. I had no power over what I ate, what I weighed, or even how I spent my time. Everything was under the control of my doctors and parents. Everything was under the control of my recovery. But the possibility of straight A's was all mine. I was the only one who could make it happen and I was the only one who impacted the outcome of my grades. It was the first thing I had complete power over in months. It was my chance to feel proud again. It was my chance to overcome the useless feeling that had become my way of life. That was why I wanted it. That was why I needed it. Perfection was my goal and reaching it was crucial.

I ended exam week hopeful. Each exam I took gave me more confidence. Each exam gave me the feeling of triumph. Nothing was set in stone but I felt as though I nailed each and every one of my exams. But, only time would tell. Anticipation settled in as the days slowly drifted away. One by one I discovered my results, each leaving me with happiness and strength, each one leaving me with an A. But, I still didn't know the results of math and science; the moment of truth was about to arrive.

First, it was math. I walked in with Meredith by my side. We shyly walked toward the teacher and anxiously asked for our results. The teacher glanced at Meredith but then settled her eyes right on me. She held my gaze as I held my breath. Worry flooded through me. I was certain the stare meant I had failed. After all, I always thought I was a failure, why should these results say otherwise. And then she spoke.

"I'm extremely surprised with you Nicole. I could hardly believe what I saw."

Oh great, I thought, *here it comes. I hate myself. I try so hard but all I can do is fail. I hate myself.*

"You..." Her voice shook me out of my thoughts and back into the classroom, "...you got a perfect score—you didn't miss a single problem. Congratulations!"

My face lit up with a smile. I could feel my hands shake and my mouth drop open. I could hear myself asking over and over again if she was serious. It had to be a joke. Maybe I was being "Punk'd." But I wasn't. I had succeeded. I was not a complete failure. For once, I felt as though I had done something right.

The feeling of pride only grew as I found out that I aced my science, history, and English exams as well. That month my report card came in the mail with an A in every box. I had done it. I received something perfect. My grades were perfect. My math exam was perfect. But something wasn't right. I still didn't feel perfect. I still had flaws. I still had improvements to make and mess-ups to fix. That's when it hit me. Perfection doesn't exist. Yet, even to this day, I still search for it with hope that I will find it. I search for it with hope that I can make it real.

Recovery

Second Semester

Recently my mom recalled a memory she had from the early days of recovery that thoroughly interested me. She told me, "I spent every day of your ninth grade year praying that you'd come home from school with fewer complaints and a slight smile."

I asked her if and when this ever happened. She answered, "I'm not sure. The change was gradual. Over time, the first words from your mouth turned into comments about homework or teachers instead of claims that you wanted to die or you hated your life. Over time, you stopped crying and giving me blank stares and started being halfway normal again."

My mom couldn't remember when these changes started. But if I had to guess, I'd say somewhere around my second semester. The recovery phase was progressing slowly, and my doctor's told me that I had finally reached a healthier weight. I returned to soccer and even got more freedom with my meals. I would begin new classes—a fresh start that would have to suffice until the fall when I would switch schools. Better yet, I had four of my eight periods with Meredith. As the semester grew closer, I began discussing the plan for school lunch with my parents. Previously I had to go home during lunch because all of my meals were supervised. But with everything heading in the right direction along with constant praise from my team of doctors, that didn't seem quite as necessary as it once had. After much discussion, and the security of knowing that Mere would be with me for lunch, they finally decided I could take over that meal on my own. I could eat food in the cafeteria with all my friends and not a grown-up in sight. Finally, they were beginning to trust me. Finally, I was beginning to gain control.

I noticed my mood lifted from the moment those lunches began. Not only did I experience freedom for the first time in six months, I also experienced a social life again. No more walking aimlessly around the school for exercise. No more hiding out in bathroom stalls and spending the hour alone. I spent each school day surrounded by a group of friends, laughing and eating like a normal teenage girl. And whenever it got difficult, I could look to my left or right and find Mere encouraging me. I started growing closer with other friends too. Some were new friends and some were old friends that I had lost touch with. No matter what the case, I knew I had found more people to count on. I never talked to them about my issue but that was part of what made our friendships so strong. I could be the new Nicole with them. I didn't feel ashamed, and I would forget about the problems that still existed in my mind and at home. Life was still hard. Life still sucked. But at least it was improving.

When my social life picked up again, it wasn't just with girls. I reconnected with my guy friends from previous years and developed a crush on someone for the first time that year. It's weird to think it took that long. In seventh and eighth grade there was always a boy I liked. I was always after someone, and often, someone was after me. But when my anorexia developed the illness became the only important thing in my life. Boys no longer mattered to me, just as friends no longer mattered to me. All I felt I needed was my eating disorder and the power of losing weight. I didn't spend time flirting with guys or even talking to them. But when second semester came around, my priorities began to shift.

My crush turned into something more. I went out with him twice in eighth grade. He was an amazing boyfriend, always showering me with compliments and listening to me no matter how crazy I was acting. But both times I had felt trapped. I don't think I was ready to be serious about someone at that point in my life. I was only fourteen and had more important things to worry about like soccer and friends. We remained close at first but lost touch throughout the summer and first semester. He had no idea how much I had struggled since we last talked. He had no idea that I had nearly died since then either. But somehow, we found our way back to each other. We didn't have any classes together besides lunch, where we sat on opposite sides of the cafeteria. I don't know how it happened, but we started texting. And then we would find each other in the halls. He was on the hockey team. He wanted me to go see him play in one of his games. Meredith, being the great friend that she is, agreed to go with me. She could tell he made me happy. And I quickly found myself liking him even more than before. He was kind, complimentary, and easy to talk to.

But there was one problem. Recovery was still taking over a majority of my life. Although I was becoming more social at school, I still didn't have the time to hang out on weekends because of my rigid food schedule. Plus, the anorexia had become a huge part of who I was and I didn't know if I could be with someone who didn't know about it, who didn't accept it. I knew that if anything were to happen between us I'd have to tell him the truth. But I was scared. I was scared he would judge me. I was scared he would laugh at me. I was scared for a week until I finally realized that if he was going to look down on me based on something so out of my control, then maybe he wasn't the person I thought he was. I decided that if he didn't take it well then it wasn't meant to be.

But it was. He listened patiently. He didn't understand it, that much was clear, but he accepted it. He liked me in spite of it and still wanted to be with me. I could tell the subject made him uncomfortable, but the conversation was successful and before long I had a boyfriend. It was just what I needed at the time. At that point, I needed to feel close to someone. I had spent months feeling alone and disconnected from the rest of the world. Second semester was looking as if it would be different. I had a variety of friends, a greater involvement in class, and a loving boyfriend. True, I still had to endure the insulting rants of my eating disorder and the daily battle with food. But the rest of my life wasn't quite so bad. It wasn't great, it wasn't even good. But it was bearable.

Soccer

My withdrawal from soccer had been abrupt and tragic to me. However, I returned gradually with less drama than I had imagined. When I first found out I couldn't play, I felt crushed, and my world was broken. But over time, the pain numbed me and the loss didn't seem quite as bad. I got used not playing. I got used to watching from the sidelines as my teammates celebrated wins. I got used to living life without soccer. I got used to it, but I never enjoyed it.

Without soccer, I felt like a part of me was missing. Soccer had defined me for so long. Gaining the ability to play again became my biggest motivation. Each day I reminded myself that eating the food would help me play. I reminded myself that surviving the struggles would lead me to my goal. I wanted life to go back to the way it was; and I needed to return to full-swing soccer mode. I thought it was just a matter of gaining weight. I thought it would take a few months. But even to this day, I'm not back completely. Instead, the decision on whether or not I can play soccer changes day to day. Some days I'm strong enough to eat extra calories, other days I'm not. Some weeks I weigh enough to exercise, others I don't. But at least I can play some days. Ever since December, the chance to play has been within my reach.

My first trips back to soccer were short-lived. In October, after regaining my period for the first time, I was allowed to play for ten minutes at the end of our last game. Those ten minutes flew by and before I knew it, I was back on the sideline, praying for the chance to have more time on the field. In November, the opportunity disappeared with the loss of more weight and of my period. When the winter season kicked up, I was allowed to play in any game if I ate enough extra calories. Physically, I was capable of playing, but mentally I was still a wreck. Over the course of the season, I only played four or five games. I was just too weak. My brain couldn't handle the overwhelming thoughts. My spirit couldn't hold off the attacks of my eating disorder. I just couldn't do it. Mentally, I wasn't ready.

Spring season was more promising. I played almost every game. It was the practices that remained a challenge. With the games it was easier to find motivation. Eating extra wasn't as impossible when I had a true desire to play. But practicing didn't hold the same excitement the games held. Therefore, pushing myself to eat for a practice was way more difficult. I scored a goal or two and had multiple assists over the course of the season, but because of the lack of practice, I could feel that I just wasn't as good as I was before. Yet my return to the sport was blissful. It was a sign that I was making progress. It was a sign that the end of anorexia was on its way.

Thinking back to the fall season when I could not play, I remember an instance that will always remain drilled in my mind. We were playing the Lightning. As I yelled and cheered from the side, I noticed a player on the other team who looked oddly familiar. I stared at her for close to five minutes, desperately trying to figure out where I had seen her. Finally, I realized where it had been—at the eating disorder clinic. I had seen her waiting for Dr. Silber. She was anorexic. She was anorexic but she was playing soccer. I was anorexic but I wasn't allowed. The moment I realized this, it didn't seem fair. I was angry that she could do something that I couldn't. I was angry that she was on the field and I wasn't. I was angry and I never forgot.

But fast-forward to the winter and our next encounter didn't upset me. That time, I too would play. It was proof of how far I had come. It was proof that I was successful. Last time our encounter left me with anger but this time it left me with pride.

Unfortunately, the pride I feel when playing soccer is often overpowered by an uncomfortable feeling. I was excited to return to soccer, but now I feel as though my passion for it has grown dim. I often wonder if I still have the drive to continue playing. A part of me doesn't, but there's still a part of me that does. I love the sport; I love talking about it and watching it. But I'm not sure if I still love playing it. Saying so fills me with sadness. It is hard because I know this feeling is a result of my eating disorder. I just can't enjoy playing soccer because I can't stop thinking about the extra food that I need to consume. I can't let loose and have fun because I feel guilty about the extra calories I have to eat. I know this isn't a good reason to stop something I love. But at the same time, I can't help it. I can't say, "Okay, I'm going to stop feeling bad when I eat extra and get over it to enjoy the game again." As much as I would love to do this, I don't have control over my feelings and thoughts. I wish I could stop, but it's not that simple. Sadly, I'm not sure if I can ever fully enjoy soccer again until my eating disorder is gone for good. I wish that would happen soon, but unfortunately, it could take years.

Like I said, the return to soccer may not have been as great as I expected. My hopes for the return were too high. My desire was too strong. But I will always remember that feeling of pride when I faced the girl for the second time and battled her on the field. I will never forget the progress I've made every second that I am on a soccer field and every second a ball is at my feet. Before, soccer was a sport. Now, it's a reward. Before, soccer was enjoyable. Now, it's complicated. Who knows, maybe someday I will regain my desire for it. Or maybe soccer will never be the same again. I wish I had the answer, but only time will tell. For now I'll just focus on doing my best and playing whenever I can.

Problems

There are a lot of problems that go along with being a self-conscious perfectionist, not to mention having anorexia and depression on top of that. With all of these traits I am nothing short of a problem magnet. Every time I felt like my life started looking up, one of these issues intervened, ruining my happiness. Even more, as soon as one intervened the others always quickly followed. It was like a domino effect.

First of all, there's the issue of self-esteem. For someone with abnormally low self-esteem like me, surviving the terrors of high school could prove even more difficult. Gossip and rumors go along with the territory of high school and can't be avoided. In a building full of hormonal, teenage girls, there will be name-calling, insulting, and talking behind people's backs. It's a fact of life. I shouldn't take it personally. I knew this, yet I couldn't stop myself from doing so. When I found out a girl called me a bitch or another girl said my outfit was ugly, it was all I can do to keep from crying. Minor insults turned into massive blows that tore me up inside. The pain came from the fact that I agreed with the comments. Each day I woke up insulting myself and fell asleep regretting my actions. It hurt when other people voiced the same insults I threw at myself. It wasn't the words that hurt me so much. It was the fact that others noticed my flaws. It was the fact that I could never reach my goal to be perfect. At that point, my perfectionism arrived in full swing. I would have given anything to be perfect; because, in my mind, I was just the opposite. It seemed like attaining perfection would answer all of my questions and solve all of my dilemmas. I pushed myself to improve, strived to be the best. No matter how much improvement I made, it never satisfied me; I was never good enough. But, I kept trying. Maybe perfection would put an end to the insults and regrets, and an end to my self-hate.

At that point my problems with anorexia and depression were constant. In my everyday life they were clearly visible and strong. But when something went wrong and took a turn for the worse, my anorexia and depression came at me with full force. For example, there was that week in the middle of second semester. That one week seemed to cause everything to fall downhill. It started with a choice.

I had been feeling more independent recently. I had been feeling more sure of myself. I still had my boyfriend and still cared about him just as much but, because of my new upbeat attitude, wasn't sure how much I needed him anymore. What I mean is this: for the past year I had depended on those around me for every little thing. I depended on others to cure me, feed me, and make me happy. Recently, I depended on my boyfriend to make me happy. But in a moment of confidence, I began to wonder if I could be happy on my own. I wondered if I could trust myself. But at the same time, I really cared for him; I couldn't just let him go because I was curious about the strength of my own independence. I was torn. I was torn for weeks until I finally made a decision. I tried my hardest to explain as I told him I needed a break, just a temporary break. I needed a chance to find the strength to be alone. That was all I wanted. But in life, things don't always go the way you want.

It broke my heart when he moved on so quickly. I felt as if I wasn't good enough. I felt as though all the lines he had fed me about caring were just lies. I felt as though my world was crashing down around me. The disappointment provided fuel for my eating disorder. Immediately, I found myself resorting back to my old ways. I spent hours thinking up plans on how to sneak in exercise or how to avoid this food or that one. I hated myself for letting this happen, and I hated myself for letting him go. My eating disorder started telling me how out of control I was. It pointed out that I had initiated the break up yet here I was crying my eyes out. I needed to regain control. My eating disorder began to spin closer to danger.

Then to make matters worse, my teacher returned the past week's math test with a giant red C marked at the top. It didn't matter that I still had a high A in that class. I didn't even remember that. All I could think of was how stupid I was for not studying more or how clueless I was for making such simple mistakes. I beat myself up about that one grade for the next several days. I pushed myself harder than ever to succeed with every piece of math homework or worksheet. I desperately searched for a way to redeem myself. The need for perfectionism was as present as ever.

Just when I thought the week couldn't get worse, I discovered another rumor and another betrayal. It seemed that every month since our friendship had ended, my ex-best friend had stirred up some drama. I couldn't get through a week without hearing about another rude comment she had made or lie she had told. The hate she had for me was obvious; and although her opinion meant nothing to me, it seemed to fuel the hate I had for myself. With the breakup, the bad grade on the test, and the vicious rumors from my once-trusted friend, my depression grew worse. Before I knew it, I was back to my suicidal thoughts and rants of hating life and wanting to die. Before I knew it, the dim light that developed during the second semester returned to complete and total darkness. I was back to feeling alone, stupid, fat, and worthless. In addition, I found out that some of my newer friends were spreading rumors about me too. They weren't the people I thought they were. It seemed as though everything I knew had become everything I didn't.

Since my devastating year began, I realized that my many disappointments caused me to lose faith. It felt as though when things were going right something always had to happen to make them go wrong again. I lost my trust in happiness. I lost my trust in hope. So much turned out unexpectedly upsetting that I began to expect sadness. I began to expect failures. That week made me feel like no one could be trusted. Yet again, I had put all my care and faith into people near me, only to be shut down. My family, Meredith, and my dog—those were the only ones I could count on, the only ones who truly cared.

Meredith

At times of tremendous suffering, we realize the luxuries we took for granted and the necessities we neglected to cherish. When life knocks us down and leaves us feeling stranded, we finally acknowledge the presence of what we formerly pushed aside. When we're stuck in a sea of darkness, we begin searching for a glimmer of light.

I like to think that Meredith was my light through the darkness of my disorder. I like to think she was my hope in the months of despair. While my other friends ran at the first sign of trouble, Meredith remained by my side. She was my best friend and my support. Her friendship served as a crucial aid throughout recovery.

I think a person's true colors show in the midst of disaster. Some claim to be brave and strong but then hide with fear as trouble develops. Some claim to have all the answers but then are speechless under pressure. Yes, I believe that disasters have to happen. They have to happen to show us who we can trust and who we can't. They have to happen to reveal the truth behind the disguises that people wear. In this way, my eating disorder was a blessing. My eating disorder taught me about myself and about my so-called friends. It taught me who was really there and who was just a fake. It taught me how lucky I was to know someone as considerate, giving, and understanding as Meredith.

Back in sixth grade, I knew her but we never talked. She was in my gym class but we followed different crowds. We had our own sets of friends. She was extremely shy while I wasn't. Her shyness prevented me from getting to know her. Thinking back, I realize what a waste that year was and how foolish I was to disregard her.

In the middle of seventh grade we grew closer. But still, she already had her set of best friends and I had mine. Sometimes we all hung out together but then returned to our own set of friends.

By eighth grade, we began turning to each other for advice. We became closer each day because of the continuous fighting between each of us and our other groups of friends. With each argument or upset, we turned to one another. We had never been in a fight with each other. We were solid friends. Yet even then, I couldn't appreciate how special

Meredith was. That appreciation didn't come until I needed it. That appreciation came at the beginning of ninth grade.

When the anorexia progressed, those girls I once considered my best friends slowly deserted me. Before my diagnosis they made fun of how "gross" I looked or how "stupid" I was for not eating more. As my diagnosis drew near, the two girls I had felt closest to abruptly shut me out. Once diagnosed, they didn't even bother to console me. In fact, I didn't even have a chance to tell them. After my diagnosis, they spread rumors. The people I cared for the most hurt me the most. At a time when I needed them they neglected me. I was left feeling alone and abandoned. But I wasn't. I wasn't alone. Meredith was there. She was there consistently and with sympathy. She never once judged me.

As my eating disorder worsened, I felt our bond grow stronger, not weaker as with all of my other friends. Because of this bond, she was the first person to whom I openly admitted I was anorexic. She was the first person I called when I was admitted to the hospital. She was the first person I told when I was forbidden to play soccer. Every life-changing discovery, every devastating event, all of it was first shared with her. And each time, I knew she would be there. I knew she would help me get through it. But her presence was subtle. She didn't overwhelm me with questions. She didn't intervene with advice. She didn't search for details or explanations. No, Meredith didn't do any of that. Instead she gave me a shoulder to cry on and an ear to confide in.

Personally, I can see why my other friends chose to run scared. I wasn't exactly the most fun girl to be around, and I never had time to hang out or talk. The eating disorder took over my life, leaving me no energy or time to keep up a social life. Staying friends with someone like me during that time must've been hard. That's why I have even more respect for Meredith. She wasn't just there for the laughter, inside jokes, sleepovers, and parties. She was also there for the tears, complaints, mental breakdowns, and heartaches. She was a friend for me, even when I couldn't be a friend to her. She was there for me, even when I wasn't there for myself. She was optimistic when all I saw was tragedy. Between us there is the bond of unconditional love. I know she will always be there for me and I will always be there for her. Best friends forever, literally.

Meredith is more than just a best friend to me, she is my hero. By that I mean she gave me a reason to live. There was one day I particularly remember when I felt extremely depressed. I was being extra hard on myself and was contemplating suicide. I had just gotten in a fight with my parents and felt as though no one cared. I was completely alone. I had to face this demon, and I was running out of strength. I began to think that death would be such an easy solution. Besides, with my parents mad at me, who would even care? And then my phone buzzed, a new text message. I opened the text and was struck with a surge of happiness. It was Meredith. It was Meredith reminding me that I wasn't alone, that someone did care. The text simply read "Hey girl! How are you? I thought I should text you because I heard that song we love on the radio and it reminded me of you. ☺" That was it. Those three sentences stopped me from following through. Those three sentences gave me a reason to live. That was how Meredith Berman, my best friend, became my hero.

Abuse

The best way I can think of to describe the complexity of my eating disorder is to compare it to an abusive relationship. The idea is similar to the idea of "divorcing" your eating disorder from the book *Life Without ED*. Like an abusive relationship, there are times when anorexia beats you down to the ground, and then there are times when it gives you comfort. It's obviously an unhealthy relationship, but it's hard to leave it. It insults you and then showers you with compliments. An eating disorder abuses you until you have to make a choice—either let it break you, or stand up and start fighting back.

As my weight went up, people began to congratulate and praise me. With each new pound and each new accomplishment, I could feel my eating disorder growing weaker and weaker. My family could see it too, and their faces beamed with joy as they watched my eating disorder slowly tumble away. I knew I should share that joy. I knew I should feel relieved that I was recovering. I knew it was a good thing. But, even to this day, I still feel alone when I think about life without my eating disorder. I still feel scared when I think about recovering. In a way, it feels like someone who I've been close to for so long has died. In a way, I feel abandoned. Now I know this sounds crazy, but let me try and explain.

When someone is in an abusive relationship, not every second of it is filled with abuse. These relationships can be filled with blissful love one minute and brutal hate the next. For the victim, they never know when the abuser will strike. The day could run smoothly while the abuser shower the victim with adoration. Then the victim says something wrong or makes a mistake and just like that, the happiness ends. Just like that, the abuser smacks her across the face. He punches her in the gut, causing her stomach to churn with pain. He slams her head against the wall leaving her dizzy and at a loss for words. It's a dangerous relationship. It's an unstable relationship. Yet, half the time it seems perfect. Half the time it seems as though nothing could go wrong. But the other half is a different story. The other half is dangerous.

My eating disorder treats me in a strikingly similar way. When I'm listening to what it tells me, I am praised and complimented. When I turn down food my eating disorder makes me feel worthy. It makes me feel untouchable. It makes me feel more loved and special. This half of my eating disorder leaves me with nothing but positive feelings. But then, there's the other half, the dangerous half. As soon as I rebel, as soon as I make a mistake or don't listen to the commands, I begin to feel the abuse. I am pounded with unbearable feelings of guilt. I am tricked into thinking I'm full, causing my stomach to bolt with pain. I am tormented with thoughts that spin out of control, leaving me dizzy and at a loss for words. I am pushed into hating myself. I am pushed into thinking I would rather be dead. The eating disorder tries to convince me to listen next time. But I know listening is unhealthy. I know the relationship is unhealthy. But at the same time, it can make me feel good. Half the time it seems as though nothing could go wrong. But the other half is a different story. The other half is dangerous.

Once a person comes to the realization that the abusive relationship must be cut from their life, following through is not easy. It can take someone years to leave their abusive husband or wife, even if they know that they need to. The struggle comes from fear. There is fear of what life alone will be like. The victim has gotten so used to having their spouse around, leaving them brings the unknown. Leaving them requires bravery. There's uncertainty about the future. That is why it's difficult. It is difficult because, as abusive as it may be, the relationship still brings the person comfort.

To be honest, letting go of my eating disorder scares me. I've become so used to the way my life revolves around it. It's what I know. It's how I live. I often question if I can make it on my own. I am scared to feel lonely. I am scared of the future. I am scared to not have my eating disorder there to solve my problems and dictate my life. But, I am choosing to be brave. Even though the future is unknown and the unknown is scary, nothing can be worse than the deadly abuse I suffer right now. And the important point for me and other abuse victims to remember is that leaving our abuser does not mean we will be alone. Leaving our abuser means we will be free. But we will still have the love of our family and friends. We will still have the support of the people who respect us. That's how I have to think of it. Life without my eating disorder is a freedom, not a loss.

But it's hard for victims stuck in an abusive relationship to cut the cord, because their significant other has become such a huge part of who they are. They love the person and they feel as though they need the person. To them, the abuser is their other half.

I sometimes feel as if my eating disorder is my other half. Over the past year and a half, being anorexic is such a huge part of who I am.

Anorexia defines me. I am anorexic and to think that one day I won't be—well that's a pretty scary thought. But the reality is that if something or someone abuses you, they don't deserve to be a part of you. They don't deserve to impact you if they can't respect you. When my eating disorder is gone I won't be an empty person, I'll be a better person.

No matter how hard it is to end an abusive relationship, it is something that needs to happen. Standing up to abuse is a choice that signifies strength and self-love.

Roller Coaster

If there's one important lesson that I've learned regarding recovery and high school in general, it's that the days are like riding a giant roller coaster. One moment you'll be at a high, feeling untouchable from the world and all of its problems. Then, before you know it, you drop down again, crashing to the ground below. The highs and lows can be overwhelming and leave you feeling dizzy, but they're just a part of life.

After breaking up with that first boyfriend during my ninth grade year, I was left at one of those lows. The confusing end of our relationship was a steep hill that I fell down fast. It left me heartbroken, with my spirits low. Nothing seemed strong enough to pull me back up again. No one seemed capable of mending my shattered heart. That's how it seemed, but I soon learned there was one boy who could.

From the moment I started talking to him, I knew we shared a special connection. We could understand each other in a way that my ex and I never could. He knew everything about me. He related to the depression and looked past the anorexia. He always knew how to make me laugh, and miraculously, he helped me move on. Suddenly, I was at the top of a hill again. The roller coaster was pulling up. It gained speed when I got A's on every test that week and began to hang out with some new friends outside of school. The week before I was upset and alone. The next week I was upbeat and surrounded by friends. It's crazy how quickly a roller coaster can change directions, isn't it?

As Memorial Day weekend grew closer, my life was running smoothly. This year, we had another soccer tournament, but it would be in a different place. Last year, the weekend in Virginia Beach had been the beginning of something terrible. But this year, I was determined to make the weekend in Gettysburg, Pennsylvania, the beginning of something amazing. With confidence, I was determined to be normal. I was determined to spend the tournament as just one of the girls. I didn't want to be reminded constantly that I was different. I didn't want to spend the time as an anorexic. To achieve this, I knew I needed to do some major convincing.

It was late May, and I had slowly gained more control over my meals. However, my parents still had control over my dinners and supervised almost everything, although not as strictly as before. But maintaining the same rigid schedule throughout the trip would only cause fighting. I had faith in myself and knew that I could handle the food on my own, but somehow I had to get my parents to have that same faith too. Everyone would feel more relaxed if they just left me alone. I could feel normal and in control, and they wouldn't have to worry about me on top of all the other stress they dealt with. Taking over my food was the obvious choice to me. Even so, my parents had their doubts. The fact that I would play three games meant I'd have to eat even more, something they weren't sure I could handle. When they brought this up, I realized they had a point. Maintaining weight would be especially hard with all of the extra exercise from playing. I was stuck. I didn't want to give up my idea, but at the same time, I didn't want to set myself up for a disaster. It was our family therapist who came up with the solution.

"Most likely, Nicole will lose weight this weekend. But what's more important is that she can push herself to gain it back. Weight loss will happen but regaining is what matters most." As he said this, I knew they were about to make a deal. Sure enough, they told me that in an attempt to give back full control, they would give me one week after the tournament to gain back all the weight I lost during it. This would build trust with my parents, and it would be an important step in recovery for me. However, if I failed, my parents would take over again, and I would take a step backward in the progress I had so recently made. No doubt about it, I was in for a tough task. I was determined; and when I set my mind to something, I'll do anything to make it happen.

Arriving at the tournament was exciting. We stayed in a luxurious hotel sharing neighboring rooms. A quaint town with shops was nearby and we enjoyed the relaxing pool area by the main lobby. Before we left, I had confided in a teammate about the goal I had at hand, and she promised to encourage and support me along the way. I spent the night giggling and laughing with the girls, almost forgetting the truth that lay beneath. I was in bliss. That first night was definitely one of those highs on my roller-coaster journey.

Another plus of our hotel was the massive swarms of cute guys who seemed to be everywhere we turned. My friend and I were walking to the pool when four or five guys came up to us and asked for our phone numbers. We talked to them for a while, exchanging names, ages, and information about our teams before continuing on our way. As we giggled my friend reminded me that we both had boyfriends at home. Joking the whole way, we met up with the rest of our team and finished off the night with a trip to the hot tub and a pit stop at the candy machine. Everything was going perfectly.

Right before I was headed to sleep, I noticed my phone begin to buzz on the table next to the window. I rushed over to check my caller ID and happily answered when I saw it was Meredith. I answered her call with enthusiasm, but she returned it with a tone of anguish that took me by surprise. Whatever she had to tell me was not good, I could tell already. Sure enough, her reason shocked me. She had gone to the movies with some camp friends that night and had seen something she thought she should share. She had spotted my boyfriend there…with another girl. As the words escaped her mouth, my roller coaster dropped down lower and faster than it ever had before. I was angry, upset, hurt and disappointed. No wonder he had barely texted me all night. Being the self-conscious girl I was, I automatically thought of reasons to blame myself. My head filled with thoughts of "I'm not good enough" and "she's better than me." As I tried to hold back my tears, a knock at the door shook me out of my shock.

I opened the door to see my teammate's smiley face shining back at me. She had come over to say good night and that she was glad I had made it to the tournament. Her enthusiasm encouraged me to move forward. Instantly, I was determined not to think about my issues at home for the rest of the weekend and to just focus on having fun. And that's exactly what I did. I had fun, and I did my best to remain normal and keep my sanity.

The first soccer game gave me an incredible rush. It was all tied up with five minutes to go. The ball was crossed to me and I had an open shot at the goal. It was tricky because I was about forty yards away from the net and I had to shoot with my left foot. But I knew we needed to score and this might be my only chance. I fired it as hard as I could and watched as it looped up over the goalie's head and into the far right corner. I stood stunned as my teammates began cheering and the parents screamed my name. We won the game and I had scored the best goal of my life. For one moment, for one brief moment, I was proud of myself. It ended up being the only goal I scored for the weekend, but it started me off with confidence. I successfully made it through lunch and dinner with memories of the game flashing through my head. My mom was barely even there to give me food orders since she spent most of the day with my brother and his team. I was bursting with a sense of freedom. And best of all, I knew I wasn't taking advantage of it.

Unlike last year's tournament, I ate a large breakfast every day and drank plenty of Gatorade. I was doing my best while still managing to make it look easy. Each meal was a struggle, but I hid my pain well. Not once did I let my eating disorder take control of me. Not once did I act out or tremble with fear. Every so often I'd think back to that phone call about my boyfriend, but as quickly as it came in, the thought shot back out. Overall, I'd say the weekend was a success.

When I returned home the real trouble developed. We were reassured that just as we expected, I had lost weight. Luckily it was only a couple of pounds. Gaining it back was totally doable, but it would take lots of focus and strength on my part. To make matters worse, I soon learned that the rumors about my boyfriend were true. Our breakup hit me hard. Just when I had gotten over one guy I had to get over the next. Relationships seemed doomed, always ending with pain and heartache. I hated myself for believing all of the lies. I hated myself for opening up. I hated myself, but for some reason, I couldn't hate him. Now that's messed up.

Needless to say, keeping strict with food that week was nearly impossible. With the disappointment that took over my life, my eating disorder grew stronger than ever. But continuously, I reminded myself of the ultimate goal. I knew that eating right was what I had to do if I ever wanted to have complete control again. I pushed myself through pain and suffering. I pushed myself until I felt ready to crumble and break. The roller coaster had fallen at the worst possible time. But I had to keep going. I couldn't get off the ride if I ever wanted to reach the end. I ate and ate. When weigh-in day came around the following Monday, I was relieved to hear that I had reached my goal. Making it through such a tough week and still coming out on top was a major turning point in my recovery. It was a step to regaining trust and respect. It was a step to showing my eating disorder that I wasn't taking its crap any longer.

The previous Memorial Day was a beginning. This Memorial Day was also a beginning. Only this time, the roller coaster was, once again, heading up.

Pride

Having anorexia is like having the same trick played on you every day. It is all one big tunnel of lies and deception. Lies the disease tricks you into thinking and lies it compels you to tell. Logic has no meaning to an anorexic. The voice of an eating disorder slowly silences the voice of reason. What makes perfect sense to an anorexic often seems ridiculous to anyone else. At the same time, what makes perfect sense to an ordinary person, often seems meaningless to an anorexic.

Eating that one cookie will make you gain weight. Seems like such an exaggerated comment, right? Wrong. To me—and all the other anorexics in the world—it is downright law, a statement to live by. Now I'm not saying that we're clueless. However I do believe we are blinded. I constantly find myself searching for answers in a room with no light, searching for reason in a world with no reality, and searching for hope on a pathway of sadness. No matter how many times I'm told that eating the cookie won't make a difference, a voice inside of me persistently tells me that it will. No matter how many times I do eat the cookie and see for myself that nothing changed, I still feel as if the next cookie, the next time, will inflate me with fat and sin.

Unfortunately, although I have made endless amounts of progress in my recovery, I still haven't found a way to shake that feeling. Staring at a cookie still terrifies me, causing me to obsess over how life altering it would be to just take one measly bite. The key is that I have learned to ignore the voice. I can tell you that I now eat cookies and other sweets on a daily basis. However, I can't say I do it without becoming drenched in guilt. Each time is a mini-horror movie. Each time my stomach drops and anxiety creeps across my body. I know what's going to happen. I know how miserable I will be and how depressed I will feel. I would give anything to avoid that atrocious sensation of anguish and guilt.

But I continue to eat those cookies. I continue to face those fears because that is where I truly have strength. That is where I truly have success. And somewhere along the way I began to feel something completely different along with my guilt and despair. I began to feel a sense of pride. Pride because I respect my body. Pride because I face my fears. Pride because I am a fighter. Pride—to feel it is worth all the pain in the world. To feel pride is to feel happiness.

My Brother Kyle

The leaves begin to change colors, and I can hear the screams of the neighborhood kids finishing out the summer with laughter and joy. One girl with pink, sparkly Skechers zooms around the cul-de-sac with a smile on her face as she shows off her new, two-wheel bicycle. Behind her, a young boy with light blond hair and a cute chubby face tags along behind her, trying to keep up on his little tricycle. All of the sudden, the boy loses his balance and falls to the ground, onto the rough cement of the sidewalk. He looks down at his knees and begins to scream and cry as he notices the scrapes that have begun to form. The moment the girl hears the cries of her brother behind her, she slams on her brakes, jumps off her bike, and quickly runs over to see what's wrong. She picks the boy up by his pudgy, little wrists and wraps him in her arms. She helps him inside and calls their mom with alarm in her voice. She stands by him as he gets the cuts washed up and bandaged. She makes sure he's okay before running back outside into the humid, August air.

Fast-forward nine years: there is the same girl, all grown up with a bright future ahead of her. But she is curled in the corner, sobbing in desperation. She has bruises on her knees from throwing herself on the hard kitchen floor. She is angry and hate dances through her eyes. She has streaks down her face, showing the paths of the tears that puddle on the seat below her. She is alone and screaming for someone to love her. All of a sudden, the boy walks in. He is much taller and his shoulders have gotten broader. He is almost a teenager now, but is mature beyond his years. He hurries over to his sister and plops down on the ground next to her. He wraps her in his arms and whispers that he loves her. He holds her hand while she lets out her emotions, constantly reminding her that it will be all right. He makes sure she's okay before running back downstairs to play Guitar Hero again.

Just over the course of this past year, it seems as though my brother has grown immensely. He's no longer my baby brother who always needed my help. Suddenly, I'm the one who needs him. Suddenly, he's the one protecting me and drying up my tears when I feel like there's no hope. I've put my family through hell because of my eating disorder. I've put my brother through the rockiest year of his life and forced him to endure many unsettling meals and witness many unsettling fights. I've managed to take up most of the time and attention of our parents, and for a long time, made it impossible for him to invite friends over to the house. I limited his year in so many ways. Yet, he didn't grow bitter. He didn't hold it against me or seek revenge. He didn't even tell me to stop or that I was annoying him. Instead, he stood by my side. He bent over backward to meet my needs. No matter how difficult life got, he stayed strong for me and he comforted me. Just over the course of one year, my brother had become more than just a cute kid who I thought of as my responsibility. Over the course of one year, my brother became my best friend.

Kyle and I had always been closer than most siblings. As far as I can recall, we never once got into physical fights and rarely got into verbal ones either. We argued occasionally over who got to watch the TV or not, but that was the worst of it. Growing up, I never understood why all of my friends complained about "hating" their brothers or sisters. I loved Kyle. I always had. But the fact that we got along was just part of my life. It seemed normal to me because that was how it had always been. It wasn't until the year of my anorexia diagnosis that I finally realized how important having a relationship like ours was. It wasn't until then that I finally appreciated him.

Kyle helped me get through recovery in more ways than one. Most importantly, he supported me, no matter what. I knew he was by my side from the moment he visited me in the hospital. As he spoke to me, I could feel the worry in his eyes. He looked as though he was about to cry and his obvious sincerity touched me. It was a blissful reminder that someone cared. It was a reminder that someone looked up to me. The second thing Kyle did was to understand. He listened wholeheartedly when I tried to explain to him what was going on in my mind. He trudged his way through many family therapy sessions and put in his advice wherever he could. When my parents were too impatient to calm me down, my brother would appear with consoling words and enormous hugs. As the months went on, I often found myself yelling out for Kyle when I was stuck in a devastating state. At times I even shut my parents away, claiming simply, "I only want Kyle!"

There was one day that I can remember where my mom made taco salad. The salad was piled with a mound of rice, a river of beans, cheese, salsa, and corn. It was massive and sent chills down my spine just looking it. I was having a particularly crummy day and the thought of eating this meal was appalling. I couldn't contain myself. I began screaming and crying and threatening to kill myself. I threw papers on the ground and stomped my feet. I tore apart the house and was left feeling desperate and embarrassed. I let my eating disorder take over and could barely even remember what had happened once I calmed down. I looked over and made eye contact with my brother. He looked stricken with fear. Right as I was about to look away, he uttered the words "I'm sorry" with regret in his voice. He began apologizing, saying that he suggested the meal; he was the one to make me feel like this. I stared at him in awe. I had just erupted and ruined our dinner. I had just forced him to listen to my squeals of anguish and fear. I had just thrown a tantrum, yet HE was apologizing to ME. In that moment, I was more thankful for Kyle than I ever had been before. Never again did I want to hear him apologize. There was absolutely nothing Kyle could be sorry for; having him around was the biggest gift in my life. Having him around was pure luck.

You could pretty much say my ninth grade year was cursed. My life seemed to be a series of unfortunate events all leading up to one enormously devastating disaster. But through it all, through all the unlucky choices and startling dilemmas, I discovered a blessing. This one stroke of luck made up for the endless amounts of misfortune that had so recently been popping up in my life. Somehow—although at times I question if I truly deserve him—I ended up with the world's most considerate and understanding brother ever.

I know I may not be the best big sister. I know I'm needy and short-tempered, and I have an evil alter ego in my anorexia. I know I can sometimes be too busy feeling sorry for myself to give Kyle all the love and gratitude he deserves. I know I'm not much of a role model, and I'm rarely ever optimistic or happy. But I love my brother with all of my heart and that's all that I can do. I have realized what a blessing he is and never again will I take my little brother for granted.

Progress

In July we planned to go to Colorado again. This trip would be different. During this trip I would eat with my family and participate. I wouldn't be cast aside because of my eating disorder, and I wouldn't get in yelling matches with my parents. I would act normal. I would be normal. I had come a long way since our last trip and I wanted to prove it. I wanted to impress everyone, including myself.

Instead of staying at my uncle's house near Denver, we decided to meet down in the mountains near Durango. We rented a house that was big enough for all of my mom's brothers, their wives, their kids, my grandpa, and his girlfriend. It was going to be a mini-family reunion and I was bursting with excitement. I was determined to succeed.

In family therapy on the weekend before our trip, we all came to a decision. The plan for the trip was that I would be in control of my own meals and for my parents to intervene only if they noticed I was eating strictly based on my eating disorder. My goal for the trip was to eat normal and appear normal. I was certain that I could handle the task. And as landed on the runway the following Saturday, the trip was headed in the right direction. We stopped in Subway without any problems and made a pit stop to pick up some groceries to bring to the house. Then we were on our way, starting the four-hour drive to Durango.

From the moment we arrived at the house I knew the week was going to be perfect. My cousins were already there and they screamed with delight when Kyle and I walked in. We were the oldest cousins there and we were their biggest source of entertainment. At the time, Kayla and Alyssa were ten- and twelve-years-old, and they looked up to both Kyle and me. But Kayla especially looked up to me. She followed me around and did whatever I did. It made me feel happy knowing that someone could see so much good in me. Then there was Jack. He was seven and a spark of energy. He was always hyper and running around. He never seemed to stop laughing or get tired, and he could put a smile on anyone's face. And then there was the newest addition to our family, Jack's baby sister Shea. She had just turned one and was the cutest baby I'd ever seen. She was the definition of precious. But my cousins weren't the only welcoming committee—my aunts and uncles were just as excited to see us. Everyone laughed and hugged. It was a joyous first night. We had fun catching up and hanging out. It was a good start to an amazing week.

Over the course of that trip, I did so many new and adventurous things. For one, my parents took me, Kyle, Kayla, and Alyssa rafting on the Animas River. It wasn't a difficult course; in fact, most of it was relatively easy. Our tour guide was friendly and the weather was nice. We got to a shallow point and the guide told us that we could jump out of the raft for a bit, but warned us the water was freezing. Of course, Kyle and I had to give it a try. We hopped into the ice-cold water and were instantly numbed. We laughed as we struggled to get back in the raft. I could barely talk; the water left me speechless. Then, because I had gone in, Kayla decided she wanted to give it a try too. She wouldn't go in alone so I had to man up and jump in again. After that we had fun getting stuck on a rock. We jumped up and down like popcorn popping trying to get the raft to move forward. We must've been stuck there for five minutes but it didn't matter. At the end of the course the rapids got rougher, and when we finished the trip we were soaking wet with giant smiles plastered on our faces.

One day, we hiked to a place called Potato Lake. My uncle is an avid fisherman so he checked the map for nearby lakes and planned out the trail we'd take to get there. It was a nice, relaxing morning. The hike was long, but not too long, and the lake was beautiful. We fished and hung out until around noon, when we headed back to the car for a picnic. It was difficult because my parents watched me extra carefully that day. They said it was because I needed to be strict because of all the hiking. I knew they were right but their comments still annoyed me.

We went to ancient cave dwellings and shopped around town. We played family poker games at night and put the downstairs foosball and pool table to good use. Then, on the last day, my aunt and I did something I'll never forget. The two of us went on a trail ride with a young girl. I had never been horseback riding before and the trail wound up a steep mountain. It was scary when we got toward the top where the trail grew more and more narrow; it was peaceful and exhilarating at the same time. The view from the top was to die for. We could see all the way to New Mexico from the top of that mountain. It was also a great time to bond with my aunt, and we couldn't have been luckier with our tour guide. That trip made me the happiest I had been in a long while.

For the majority of the stay in Durango, I felt like I did a really good job of being normal. I ate every meal with the rest of the family and never screamed or made a fuss. I was flexible when my cousins wanted to go out for ice cream by switching the times of my dessert and snack so I could join them on their midday treat. I chose cereals that sounded good to me and drank the drinks I wanted to drink. I came across calm and collected around food and was able to turn off my anxiety. I felt as though I was accomplishing a lot. However, my parents still seemed worried. They would pull me aside and tell me their concerns, abruptly interrupting my blissfulness. They would remind me I was anorexic by commenting on how low something was in calories. They told me I would lose weight, but at that point, I didn't even care. I was finally happy. I finally knew what it felt like to be a normal teenager. Letting this feeling last for as long as possible was worth all the work I'd have to do to gain weight when I got back. I made this clear. And when I spoke, I sounded just as genuine as I felt. My parents tried to understand. They backed off and let me eat the best I could, with the agreement that I needed to regain whatever weight I lost during the trip. But I wasn't worried. Besides, I was eating normal amounts. I was eating five times a day. I was eating enough so that, if I did lose weight, it wouldn't be too much.

That Thursday, we all felt torn about leaving. The rest of the family was staying another day and we desperately wanted more time as well. But on the other hand, my mom had already made plans for us to go see the Grand Canyon before heading home. So even though we wanted to stay, we decided we'd rather leave and continue on our journey. We packed up and said good-bye with a million good memories. I took back the most. I took back the feeling of being happy. I took back the knowledge that there can be life after my anorexia. I took back pride from being surrounded by little cousins who looked up to me. I took back love because my family had given me plenty of it. I took back more of Nicole and less of the eating disorder. The trip was so different from our last one, just another sign that I was making progress.

Grand Canyon

As I approached the vast canyons and looked out at the vigorous blue sky above me, I realized that it had been almost a year since beginning the painful journey of recovery. Twelve months earlier I was carefree and living in happy oblivion. Eleven months earlier I was diagnosed, still not fully understanding. Ten months earlier I was confined to a hospital bed, clinging for my life. And then I stood in front of the Grand Canyon taking it all in. And by all, I don't mean just the sights around me, although of course I was compelled to take in the view, the hot but humid-less weather, and the noise of others' exclamations as they too looked out at the wondrous land below. But I also took in that past year. Those long days followed by those hard nights. The weight gains along with the weight losses. Remembering everything good while still remembering everything bad.

And then it hit me. It is the reason I could only think of that year as I looked out at the miles and miles of beauty. It was because they were alike in so many ways. Now at that point I imagine you're feeling confused as you think *how could she compare something as magnificent as the Grand Canyon to something as villainous as anorexia?* And don't get me wrong, I agree. I would be lying if I said they didn't have plenty of major differences. But yet, if you look closely, it is clear that strikingly significant similarities lay within.

Looking out at the Grand Canyon gave me chills. It was the idea that something could be so big, but so small at the same time. As I looked out I felt like a speck of dust in a large room. The canyon seemed to stretch its arms endlessly in every direction. It was bigger than I could've ever imagined. But then I remembered—it was only a fraction of our country. And then, our country was only a fraction of the world. And amazingly, the world was only a fraction of the universe. This cycle could go on and on. Compared to me the Grand Canyon was huge, but compared to the world it was merely a tiny dot on a map. And that's when my thoughts traveled to the only other thing that had made me feel this small before. My anorexia. The disease overwhelmed me, overwhelmed my life. It engulfed me with its lies, deception, and chaos, as if I was a small motorboat trapped in a horrendous hurricane. The problem made me feel as if nothing else in the world mattered, and no one else could ever understand my pain. Yet, taking a step back, it was clear that it was only another deception. Because in reality there were so many people in the world, each one fighting their own battle, each one feeling as though getting through the struggle was the most important task in the world. But how could that be true? How could one girl's problem of what new shoes to buy compared to another's problem of how to make amends with their best friend? But then how could making up with a friend compare to battling anorexia? And how could battling anorexia compare to living in Africa, starving to death, being homeless, and battling AIDS, all at the same time? The answer? It can't. While my problem may seem huge to me, there are bigger problems out there waiting to be solved. Like the Grand Canyon, the problem of anorexia was both big and small depending on how you looked at it.

But, that's not the disease's only deception. While I recovered, I tried to hide my pain by plastering a smile across my face and letting my laughter ring through the ears of my friends. To them, I was just as happy as always, if not happier. Little did they know, while I appeared to be at peace on the outside, there was nothing short of a war raging on the inside. I figured the Grand Canyon fools its spectators in the same twisted way.

I looked out and felt a cool breeze hit my face. I heard birds chirping to each other and I watched as they swooped down, landing on the edges of the canyon. Below me I see the calm river and around me I can only see smiling faces. The canyon had everyone believing there was nothing but peace and happiness within its walls. However, just a few hours later my family and I scurried into an air-conditioned building to cool off and watch a movie on the canyon. As I watched the movie, I witnessed a different side of this tremendous land. The movie displayed scenes of torturous rapids and vicious animals. A mountain lion attacked a man. A waterfall grasped a traveler, dragging him out of his boat. A poisonous snake slithered around waiting for his prey. It all seemed so scary, chaotic, and destructive. Like anorexia, the canyon appeared hopeful and peaceful while still holding vicious troubles within.

Surprisingly, the most crucial similarity also happens to be the one I most often forget. As I gazed out, I thought to myself that the canyon seemed endless. But deep down, I knew there was an end. Just one week earlier I was back home in Maryland, with no canyons in sight. The process of recovery was no different. There were times when a sense of desperation took over. I would lose all hope and struggle to get through every day. The constant battle going on in my head seemed unbeatable and I felt as though the pain would never end. But deep down, I knew there was an end. Just one week earlier I was looking forward to vacation, joking around with my friends, and briefly experiencing happiness. And although it was hard for me to believe, one day, happiness would visit me more and more often. One day, happiness would take over, and the struggle and pain of recovery would end.

Freedom

Finally I got some freedom. Finally I had my own responsibilities. Finally I had gained the trust of my parents. Getting their permission to go on the beach trip in August of 2008 with Meredith and her family meant more to me than anyone would ever know. For one week, loud, happy people would surround me. For one week, I would be carefree. For one week, I would be normal. It would be a preview of the many beach trips to come. It would be a preview of life after anorexia.

From the moment we arrived in Bethany Beach, Delaware, the four of us were undoubtedly pumped. It was me, Mere, her sister Meg, and her sister's best friend, Amy. We sat in a circle on the top floor of a model house. Meredith's parents were in the process of buying a beach house so they needed to make a pit stop at the realtor's office. Besides being an office, the realtor had a model home for customers to tour. When we arrived, the four of us ran up the stairs and made ourselves at home in the "hang out room" in the middle of the upper floor. We kicked off our shoes and plugged in the iPod speakers. We put on *Finding Nemo* and busted out the games. *Apples to Apples* was the name. I had never heard of it before but the other three girls assured me it was fun. The rules: you picked five cards and from those cards you chose the noun that you thought would go best with the adjective that was placed in the middle at the start. Then, one person judges the best combination and the person they pick gets to be the judge next round. At first it sounded a little boring. But the more we played the more I laughed. Our combinations got sillier and sillier as the game went on and we backed up our choices with hilarious explanations.

I'll never forget Amy's face when she judged the word "reliable." I had chosen "Jupiter" as my noun and she asked why the second she saw my pick. In reality, I had no real reason for choosing it, but none of my other cards had been any better. I thought fast, trying to come up with something clever. Before I knew what I was saying I heard, "Well…because you can always count on Jupiter to be in our galaxy!" The others stared at me and then burst out laughing. The craziness just kept on coming after that. We yelled and giggled and sang as we sat in the model home in a neighborhood by the beach. One of our select "beach week songs" blasted through the iPod speakers and we got up to have a little dance party. We bounced around and sang our hearts out. We only stopped when Mere's mom rushed up to tell us there were buyers about to come up to tour the model home. We tried to settle down but we were still a bit out of hand when the startled buyers walked up the steps.

"Are you part of the model," one buyer asked, causing us to erupt into more uncontrollable laughter. We stayed up there for hours, without a care in the world. And when the realtor brought us a plate of freshly baked chocolate chip cookies, I even let myself have one. And I didn't eat it as part of a meal or in substitute for something else. No, I had already eaten breakfast and I knew I was about to have lunch. I took the cookie because I wanted it. I took the cookie because I was normal and because that's what everyone else did. It was a signal to my eating disorder that this trip was about doing whatever I wanted. This trip was about having fun.

We spent most of our next few days tanning on the beach and fooling around in the water. We only went back inside to eat lunch or use the bathroom. The atmosphere was so relaxed that I don't think I felt anxious or worried once. Sometimes my thoughts drifted back to food but it was easy to push them away. It was easier to relax that week at the beach than any previous time since my anorexia had developed. Another perk of being at the beach was the group of positive, loving people I had surrounding me. Mere, Meg, Amy, and I all got along and could spend hours hanging out and joking around. Mere's parents were hilarious and easy to talk to. They looked out for us all but managed to provide us with plenty of laughs at the same time. I think of the Berman's as my second family, and that includes Amy. Each one of them is hilarious, kind, and supportive. Each one of them cares. The atmosphere they created at dinner was the funniest I ever witnessed. We had so many inside jokes by the end of the trip and so many good memories.

In the beginning of the week, everyone got kicks out of teasing me about my lack of a tan. I accepted the fact that I was extremely pale. It wasn't my fault though! I blamed my dad. But they wouldn't tease me for long. I made it a mission to get a tan line during the trip. Of course, Meredith's parents made sure I regularly applied sunscreen so that I wouldn't get burned. And it worked. Halfway through the week I was praised for my increasingly browner tan line. It was fun for them to track my success in the sun based on how pale I was throughout the week.

Tanning and hanging out on the beach filled most of our days, but that wasn't all we did. The first night of our vacation, we went mini-golfing and out for ice cream. And, believe it or not, I ate ice cream. I didn't sit there watching them enjoy the sweet, melting dessert; I treated myself to a scoop as well. I was doing everything in my power to prove to my eating disorder that I hadn't forgotten my goal for the week. I was still in control and nothing was going to change that. The next night, we went into a neighboring beach town. We walked around and explored the shops before heading home to make yogurt parfaits and play a game called *Taboo*. The game turned out to be our favorite game that week. It was all we did in our spare time. Just like *Apples to Apples* it was a game that constantly left us entertained and laughing. The only problem was that Meg and Amy knew each other really well. For the game, you have to pair up and knowing your teammate gives you a huge advantage. Mere and I knew each other really well but we hadn't been best friends for five years like the other two had. In spite of that, the game was still fun and turned into a huge Berman family addiction.

We also took advantage of the house's massive TV and the multiple movies we had brought from home. We stayed up late watching old movies, comedies, and a lot of chick flicks. Poor Dave—Mere's dad suffered through them all. But deep down, we all knew he enjoyed it. We even went shopping a couple of times; however, we couldn't coerce Dave into joining us on those trips.

As the week came to a close, more lively visitors joined our company. Karen, Mrs. Berman's best friend, and Minnie, Mere's grandma, both drove down to join us for Meredith's fifteenth birthday. The atmosphere in the house got wilder and crazier when they arrived. The house was filled with love and excitement, family and friends. I was honored to be included. I didn't think about anything eating-disorder-related that week. They treated me like I was normal and I felt like I was normal.

On Meredith's birthday night, she requested to go to dinner at a restaurant she loved. That was the only night I noticed my eating disorder trying to butt its way into my decisions. I worried over the menu when it was time to order. There were so many options and everything was so unknown. Everyone was talking about splitting this and getting that and talking about the chocolate cake that was coming later. I felt scared. I felt anxious. This was the only part of the vacation when I wished I could go home. I decided to order a salad as my main dish. It was the only option that jumped out at me. It wasn't until the minute the waitress asked for my order that I realized that was not a choice made by me. My eating disorder would order a salad. I changed my mind and picked the first fish I saw on the menu and that was that. I ordered Chilean Sea Bass and I enjoyed it too. The reminders of my anorexia's existence were brief. As soon as the menus were out of the way I centered myself back to the table. I joined in on the teasing and laughing and screaming. I joined in the celebration of the anniversary of the day my best friend was born.

When Saturday came around it was time to leave. We ended our last minutes in the house by taking a group picture. We set three cameras on self-timers but only two pictures were taken. It was Karen's camera that was accidentally put on video. We all stood there arm in arm in front of the beautiful, yellow house on the calm, peaceful beach. The sun shone down and the memories of an unforgettable week were etched in our minds. I looked around and beamed. I realized that life was going to be all right. I was surrounded by people who loved me; and when I returned home to my family, the love would remain. I was able to act normal and I figured out what I wanted to do. So what if recovery wasn't over? Maybe it never would be. Maybe I would battle this disease for many years to come. But in that moment, I didn't care. I was happy and that was all that mattered. I looked at my surroundings and realized that the world seemed at peace finally. My life was looking up, and I was positive that I was capable of coming out on top.

Struggles

There are so many different kinds of struggles. There are personal struggles and team struggles. There are private struggles and open struggles. There are mini-struggles, huge struggles, short struggles, and long struggles. There are so many different kinds of struggles, but no matter what, a struggle is always hard.

My anorexia encompassed just about every kind of struggle you can imagine. I mentally battled with myself to try and make the right choices. I had to fight on my own, yet there were times when I needed help. In these instances, recovery was a team struggle, each member of my family joining together to beat the eating disorder. I had to make some tough decisions where only I knew the struggle behind them. But there were many times where my agony was clear. For example, when I screamed and cried and threw myself on the floor my struggles were obvious. I worked toward little goals like playing soccer again, getting my period, getting to a certain weight, and finding the courage to eat a certain food. The main goal, however, was much bigger. The main goal was to discover and accept myself. The biggest goal was to establish an eating-disorder-free lifestyle. Sometimes, my issues with meals were temporary. I'd get upset and fight it but then I would sit down to eat within ten minutes. Other days, we were not as lucky. Depending on the food or my mood, meals could last up to two hours. The struggle to eat would not let up, and my feelings of frustration remained. I struggled with every day, every meal, every goal, and every problem. And none of it was easy. No part of recovery was easy.

No matter who you are, you will have to face your own struggles. Nobody's perfect. As much as I try, deep down I know that I cannot attain perfection. We all make mistakes. And each mistake leads to a struggle. Each mistake causes a problem that requires work to fix. Some people make big mistakes like cheating on a spouse, robbing a bank, or getting sucked into anorexia. These mistakes bring the hardest struggles. You have to work hard for forgiveness, go to prison, or fight to recover. But other mistakes aren't quite as drastic. Some are as simple as failing a math quiz, losing a soccer game, or forgetting to buy lemonade at the grocery store. These struggles are not as devastating or time-consuming.

These mistakes can be righted if a person studies again, practices more, or adds another errand to the to-do list. Either way, the struggle requires extra effort; it's never easy.

The way I see it, life is just a series of struggles. Each day brings a new one. After each one is overcome, another one is found. People will always have struggles to deal with. Maybe that's the point. Maybe the point of living is to overcome the struggles. Maybe the point of living is to face the struggles and figure out a way to use them. The point of living is to follow the struggles and figure out who you're supposed to be. The struggling is all one messed-up path that leads us to our purpose.

Hope

In the past year, I found that hope can solve any problem, no matter how destructive or wounding it is. Without hope, the suffering will never end. Without hope there is no chance of making it through. Hope is more powerful than knowledge and strength. Hope is more important than luck or skill. I believe hope is the most important feeling of all.

You need three qualities to have hope. First, you need patience. In times of turmoil, we often feel desperate to escape and return to the security we once had. But getting over a problem takes time. When a family member dies, mourning lasts longer than a day. The healing process takes time, and the grief never disappears. Yet over time, if you're patient, you begin to accept the death, even though it will always make you sad. When a boy you love breaks up with you, you can't get over him just like that. Mending a broken heart takes time. As you begin to get used to life without him, you will move on, even have a crush on a new guy although you will always have distant feelings for the last. When I was diagnosed with anorexia, I couldn't recover right away. Recovery is a long and painful process. But one day, as my power over the disease grew stronger, I started to enjoy food, even though I will still have mild feelings of guilt. Without patience, there is no hope. If you expect a quick solution you will be disappointed. As a result of disappointment, you may lose all hope.

The second crucial step to finding hope in the midst of despair is determination—the will to reach a goal. You need the drive to succeed and the strength to do whatever it takes. For me, I was determined to play soccer again. Each pound I gained and each meal I ate were steps to reaching that goal. When it got hard and I felt as though I couldn't continue on, I reminded myself that I needed to hang in there if I ever wanted to sprint down that field again. The drive to regain this huge part of my life helped me find a reason to work through the pain. More importantly, it gave me something to look forward to. And looking forward to something gave me hope. When I reached that first goal, I shortly set another—eat ice cream. Then I aimed to eat at a restaurant, maintain my period, and take back some food control. I kept my determination up by setting frequent goals. As a result, I found hope that one day, when all was over, I'd be happy again. Reminding myself of these goals daily provided me with consistent surges of hope and encouraged me through the toughest of days.

The last trait you need to maintain hope is optimism. I find this step the hardest to take. In fact, optimism is hard for anyone to find while going through a life-altering disaster like anorexia. When each day is grim and seemingly worse than the day before it, optimism is nearly impossible. When everything seems to go wrong, how can you believe that one day something will go right? During recovery, I was often told that one day it would all be over. I was told that they wouldn't make me gain wait forever. I was told that one day I would feel happy eating cakes and pizzas and burritos. I was told that one day I'd regain the power to decide what I ate and when. But at the time, it didn't seem like any of that was possible. I felt the quest to gain weight would never end and that eating cake was a nightmare I would never overcome. My parents told me exactly what to eat every day; I couldn't believe that one day I would choose for myself.

Life was torture and they wanted me to believe that it would get better. They wanted me to be optimistic. But finding the good in things was difficult. Happiness was overshadowed by sadness and negatives canceled out the positives. For the first few months I didn't even try. I had absolutely no optimism; therefore, I believed that there was no way I would survive anorexia. I believed that my life would go on the same way unless I finally killed myself or starved to death. I had no hope because I had no optimism. But when I witnessed day in and day out the happiness of my peers, something inside of me finally clicked. That—along with the introduction to several recovered (and happy) anorexics—finally caused me to feel more optimistic. I saw that others got through their issues, so why couldn't I? As my optimism grew, so did my hope. Then, as the hope grew, my feelings of suicide slowly shrank away.

It wasn't until I found hope that I finally decided to be free. It wasn't until I found hope that I decided I no longer wanted my eating disorder or that I no longer wanted to suffer. When I found hope, I found the promise of a better life. When I found hope, I thought of my future as something to look forward to, not something to avoid. Hope that I could get through made me think of life after the anorexia. I started thinking about what I wanted to do, where I wanted to go and who I wanted to meet. I started thinking about what college I'd go to or what career I'd pick. Most importantly, I started thinking about the person I wanted to become. I wanted to be smart, generous, and understanding. I wanted to be confident, brave, and fun loving. I wanted to be adventurous and social. I wanted to be better. Finding hope taught me that there is more to life than being skinny and there is more to me than being anorexic.

Beginning of the End

When all was said and done, it would seem as though that year was the worst of my life. Think about it: slowly starving myself, almost dying, spending a week in the hospital, enduring long months of recovery, experiencing brutal fights with my parents, contemplating suicide, being betrayed by my closest friends, getting my heart broken…twice, being gossiped about constantly, and feeling immense guilt after every single meal. In so many ways that year was the ultimate worst. But in an odd way, I almost feel blessed to have been put through it. That doesn't mean I enjoyed the year, because there was no part that I considered fun. But it did mean that I had learned to accept it.

Of course there are plenty of moments when I am filled with regret. I think about the choices I made and wonder *what if…* There are so many times when I scold myself for choosing the friends I chose or following the paths I followed. Maybe if something had gone differently, I wouldn't be here right now. Maybe I'd be happier. But the past can't be undone and I can't change what has already happened. Besides, I've come to the conclusion that everything really does happen for a reason. I choose to believe that this was meant to happen to me. I was meant to end up here. I was meant to learn the lessons this disease has taught me. I was meant to recover and write this book. I was meant to inform others about the truth. I was meant to battle with anorexia.

With each mental breakdown, I grew stronger. With each month I survived, I grew braver. And with all of the suffering combined, I have a better perspective on life in general. I'm no longer the girl who obsesses over shopping at the right stores or having the right friends. I'm no longer the girl who takes for granted all the perks she was born with. I'm no longer the girl who looks past the sick, old woman in the street or the obviously depressed mother that passes by in the grocery store. I have gained a new sympathetic eye. I feel for those with pain because now I can relate to what they're feeling. I appreciate my home and freedoms because I pay more attention to those without such luxuries. I have stopped caring so much about what others think because I have gained a new independence. I have discovered who I am. I have found myself.

Before the eating disorder I was just the friend. I was a soccer player. I was a follower. I was, in my eyes, "the ugly one." During the eating disorder I was just an anorexic. I was a loner. I was insane. I was, in my eyes, "the fat one." But now, as the eating disorder continues to lose its strength, I am finally becoming Nicole. I am starting to see myself for who I really am. I am a writer. I am understanding and have a desire to give. I am, in my eyes, "the courageous one."

And to prove that I have begun to find myself, I decided to take on a new look. This new look reflects my new identity. This new look shows that I am happier. It shows that I am prouder. Earlier this morning, my mom took me back to that same hair salon that had dyed my hair near-black eight months before. Only this time, I wasn't there to look darker. This time, I was there to get highlights, blond highlights.

But even though my hair is brighter to symbolize the positive improvement that has come along in my life, I still suffer. Generally, I am happier and stronger. I have learned how to take charge and beat down my anorexia. I have learned how to mildly enjoy food and make choices based on what I want, not what my eating disorder wants. I have discovered who I am and have found hope in my life. But, my problems have not disappeared. Every day is still a struggle. Every meal is still a hurdle. I still hear the voice of my eating disorder, but I am learning to ignore the voice. I am learning to silence it and continue on.

My recovery isn't over and I'm not sure if it ever will be. But finally I am sure that my life will go on. I have found people to live for and goals to reach. At times, I still feel alone. I know that many people still do not understand me. The difference is that now I understand myself. And because of that, I no longer feel completely misunderstood.

Made in the USA
San Bernardino, CA
22 October 2013